AF469499

ONE MAN AGAINST THE DRYLANDS

PEGGIE BENTON

ONE MAN AGAINST THE DRYLANDS

Struggle and Achievement in Brazil

COLLINS AND HARVILL PRESS
LONDON 1972

ISBN 0 00 262608 X

Set in Monotype Bembo

Made and Printed in Great Britain by
William Collins Sons and Co Ltd, London and Glasgow

for Collins, St James's Place and
Harvill Press, 30A Pavilion Road,
London SW1

CONTENTS

ILLUSTRATIONS

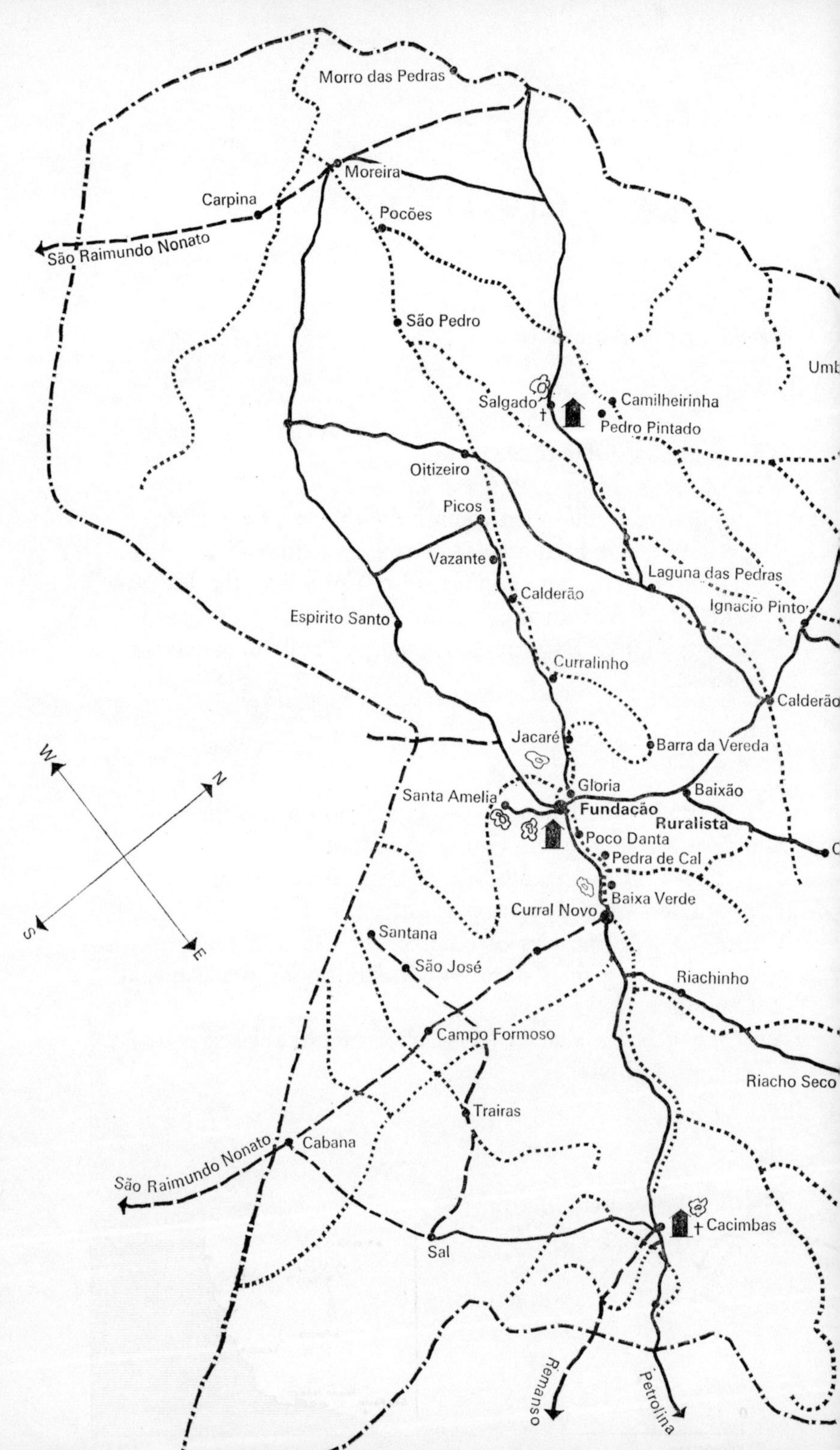
Morro das Pedras
Moreira
Carpina
Pocões
São Raimundo Nonato
São Pedro
Umb
Salgado
Camilheirinha
Pedro Pintado
Oitizeiro
Picos
Vazante
Calderão
Laguna das Pedras
Ignacio Pinto
Espirito Santo
Curralinho
Calderão
Jacaré
Barra da Vereda
W
N
Gloria
Baixão
Santa Amelia
Fundacão
Ruralista
Poco Danta
Pedra de Cal
Baixa Verde
Curral Novo
S
E
Santana
São José
Riachinho
Campo Formoso
Riacho Seco
Trairas
Cabana
São Raimundo Nonato
Cacimbas
Sal
Remanso
Petrolina

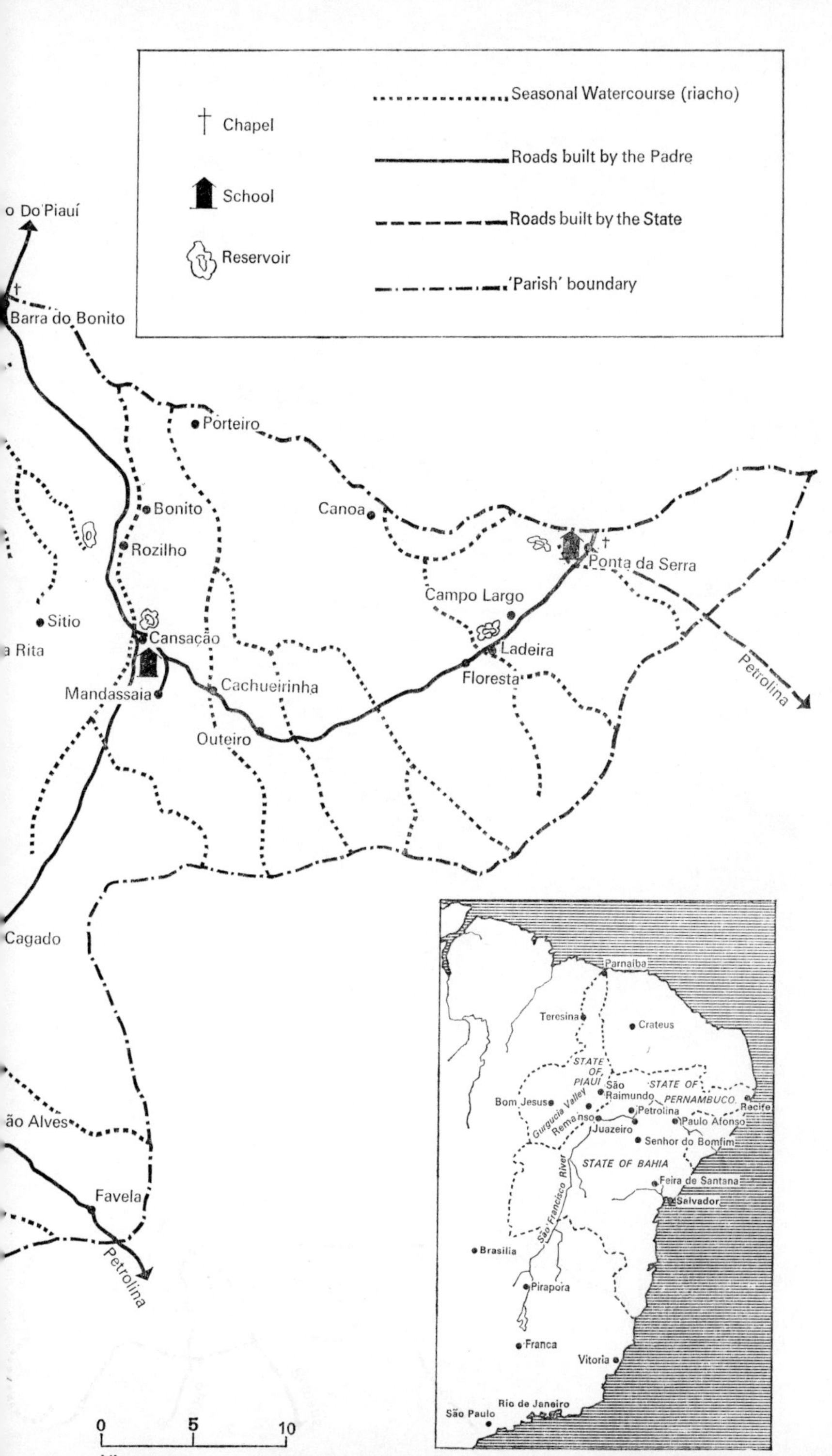

Seasonal Watercourse (riacho)
Chapel
Roads built by the Padre
School
Roads built by the State
Reservoir
'Parish' boundary
o Do Piauí
Barra do Bonito
Porteiro
Bonito
Rozilho
Canoa
Ponta da Serra
Campo Largo
Sitio
Cansação
a Rita
Ladeira
Floresta
Mandassaia
Cachueirinha
Petrolina
Outeiro
Cagado
ão Alves
Favela
Petrolina
0
5
10
kilometres
Parnaíba
Teresina
Crateus
STATE OF PIAUÍ
São Raimundo
STATE OF PERNAMBUCO
Bom Jesus
Gurgucia Valley
Remanso
Petrolina
Recife
Juazeiro
Paulo Afonso
Senhor do Bomfim
STATE OF BAHIA
São Francisco River
Feira de Santana
Salvador
Brasilia
Pirapora
Franca
Vitoria
Rio de Janeiro
São Paulo

PART ONE

A Distant View

1

THE sky was like a great gleaming bowl upturned over the silence of the dry lands. The sun stood so high that the spiked shadows of the cactus radiated from their stems like short black roots. This was the *caatinga* in the 'Polygon of Drought' which stretches behind the verdant coasts of North-East Brazil.

To the east and west, on the rim of the horizon, two plumes of dust rose and wavered towards one another.

The jagged shadows had lengthened and tangled before the dust plumes, tall now and choking, approached the dry bed of the *riacho*, where water only flowed during the rains. On the east bank horsemen in leather jerkins and chaps pranced in a cloud of dust. Beneath the tasselled and strapped leather hats they raised gnarled faces to the sky and, with reins gathered high in the left hand, flung wide the other arm and fired a volley of greeting into the air.

Beyond the riacho a single figure on a gaunt beast emerged and slowly clarified against the opposing dust cloud – the Padre on his raw mount, the pale tropical cloth of his cassock stained and tattered. Meagre living and long hours on horseback under the merciless sun had made his stocky body as tough as the twisted boughs of the caatinga and his pock-marked face like worn leather. His air authoritarian but compassionate, the dark eyes set in a web of fine lines, he surveyed the plunging horsemen and signed to them to save their precious cartridges.

This was one more encounter during the annual *desobriga* when the priest, by ancient tradition, rode through his parish, giving his people the opportunity to discharge their obligations towards the Church.There was no road in all the 3,000 square miles of the parish, but following tracks through the *mato*, or scrub, he would stop in each hamlet, usually of half a dozen primitive houses, so that the people could come for baptisms or marriages and celebrate a mass which they did not understand but vaguely felt to be beneficial. Deaths and burials seldom occurred to fit the rhythms of the annual visit.

The Padre would be followed by a sacristan with the necessities for the mass in his saddle-bags, and a *tropeiro* to carry the food and look after the animals. Behind came a miscellaneous group – a couple of pedlars with cartridges and bags of salt and sugar, some coffee, a demijohn of *cachça* cane spirit, a few combs and trinkets. At a respectful distance straggled a prostitute or two, dusty and travel-worn but strong and willing as an enduring mare.

Money was scarcely used in the caatinga and for isolated hamlets this might be the only time in the year when a few coins could be spent. The simple foodstuffs were produced at home or bartered with a neighbour. Cartridges, a necessity, were bought after the sale of an animal, if it could be driven far enough to be sold without shedding too much flesh, or the skin of a goat pegged out in the sun to dry beside its meat which, once it was leather hard, would be consumed over a period of weeks by the family.

All household equipment was made at home and the fire lit with flint and tinder. This was the life of the Middle Ages in an isolated and backward land. But the year was 1958.

Little had changed since the Jesuit Fathers in the seventeenth century led the Portuguese settlers into the interior, building small chapels and setting up lonely crosses as they advanced. Life was hard, but often no harder than the serfdom of Portugal. There, the peasants had glimpsed magnificence on feast days, but here they were their own masters with legal title to a land so poor that no one would want to take it from them. The Jesuits were a link with the world outside and with the next. People were familiar with the rhythms of the religious year, with stories of saints and angels, with the Mother of God and her Son, and the cloudier concept of the Trinity. But when the Jesuits were expelled in the eighteenth century the constant contacts were lost and the caatinga became a forgotten place.

Two hundred years later, the people of the caatinga were still free, with no absentee landlords to skim the meagre yield from the land, but free to starve and die in the terrible cyclic droughts which scourge an area already parched.

The sudden tropical darkness fell as the small troop led the priest up a stony rise to a group of huts. In the flickering light of wicks placed in clay saucers he could see the women with their children clustering around. Most seemed old, though probably in years they were not, since hardship and childbirth allowed them an average life span of only thirty-three years. Many of the smaller children were naked, in spite of the chill of nightfall, since modesty was the most important consideration in sharing out the meagre supply of clothing and their nakedness would not offend.

In the yard of the largest hut a pot was bubbling on the fire. The women bowed in welcome and the Padre was offered a stool, his saddle-bags were hung by the door and his mount tied with others beneath a stunted tree.

When the last bone had been thrown to a dog – for this was a special day and there was meat amongst the black beans – hammocks were slung. The Padre, an honoured guest, must sleep beneath a roof with his hosts, hammocks close-slung, while the children tossed and snuffled on the skins laid for them on the floor. He might long for the clear air outside beneath the stars, the silence broken only by the harsh cry of a night bird or a rustle in the dry leaves, but decorum must be observed and he must breathe the staleness of tired bodies, disturbed by the noises of their sleep.

The fires turned cold and the beasts grew quiet. Here and there, a man, inflamed by the fiery cachaça, stole away into the mato to a more pleasurable mount, and the long ropes of a hammock groaned under the double load.

2

PADRE MANUEL LIRA PARENTE was born in 1923 at Bom Jesus in the State of Piauí, which hangs like a leech from its narrow hold on the north-east coast of Brazil. It is the poorest of the States, and becomes poorer and emptier as one goes south towards the arid scrubland of the caatinga.

His family, the Parentes do Rey (or 'Kinsmen of the King'), emigrated from Portugal in the eighteenth century and settled in the North-East to become landowners and officials. An orphan at seven, the young Manuel was sent to the Benedictine Seminary in Salvador de Bahia and left it to become a priest in the prelacy of São Raimundo Nonato, a drab little town with unpaved streets and two thousand inhabitants, on the edge of the caatinga.

Although it lies in the *agreste*, a less desolate part of South-East Piauí, which though dry can still produce cash crops, São Raimundo is isolated. Its only link with the State capital, Teresina, is a two-day journey over dirt roads. The region's natural outlet to the fertile lands and the big cities is through Petrolina and Juazeiro, either side of the São Francisco River, 125 miles away. But these towns belong respectively to the States of Pernambuco and Bahia which are not interested in improving conditions in Piauí.

Whilst riding out on the desobriga the Padre realised that if São Raimundo was cut off, the caatinga was far more so, and felt itself to be completely abandoned by Federal and State Governments alike. With minimal production and purchasing power, tax returns were negligible and its only interest to politicians was as a possible source of votes. But since the ability to write one's name is a qualification for voting in Brazil, and these people were illiterate, there was nothing to be gained by giving them their due. So, though a trickle of the money allotted for education, medical services, road building and so on reached the agreste, in the caatinga there were no schools and no religious care but the annual desobriga; a doctor or midwife had never been seen, and there was only an occasional dirt road in the whole vast area.

Nature, too, deals harshly with the caatinga. Night and day are subject to an unchanging rhythm. All the year round blazing sun and chill darkness slice the equatorial day in half. For months on end no rain falls, but in a normal season, at some time between November and May, torrential rains turn every dry watercourse into a raging spate. After the rains the caatinga flushes with a fugitive green between the greys of the cactus. Each family plants its patch of manioc and black beans for the following year, close-fenced against the marauding goats. If all goes well, in three months the crop is ready to be stored and eked out until next planting time. But sometimes the rains are too light to soak the ground deeply and the seeds wither and are lost.

In a normal year, by the end of July, the landscape of the caatinga has turned to a tracery of thorns and branches bleached like bones against the radiant, empty sky. The cattle eat the dry leaves or are fed on the leathery foliage of the occasional *juazerio* tree or on cactus, scorched in the fire and stripped of its thorns, while the voracious goats will tackle the cactus, spines and all. To round up the cattle the men of the caatinga, leather-clad and with their tough leather hats strapped under their chins, have to charge head-down through the spiny brush.

Gradually the river beds dry out to leave pools which shrink into muddy wallows. But in the sub-soil there is water, bitter and brackish and griping the bowels, and for this wretched liquid many women will walk for miles to carry a tin home on their heads.

With the rains comes hope, but the grimmest ordeal of the year. Roots which were previously edible turn poisonous in the damp; game becomes scarce and the downpour brings a chill which puts an edge on hunger and strikes through the shrunken covering of the flesh. Somehow, the people cling to life and hope, supported by the high-protein milk and cheese of the good months, which make their normal diet the best of any backward rural area in Brazil.

But once in a decade or so, no rain falls. The precious livestock must be killed, grudgingly, to maintain life. There are some bitter roots which can be scraped and chewed to give a little comfort to the belly. Finally, according to the historic pattern, when the last animal has been slaughtered and the clay storage pots are empty, a thorn bush is dragged across the gap in the compound fence. The family makes its way across the stony ground to the distant highway, the wife carrying some bedding and the latest baby, unless her burden has been lightened by one of the shallow graves along the way. With luck they will be picked up by a 'parrot's cage' truck (so-called because of the wooden lattice which prevents the standing passengers from being thrown out during the days of jolting over the rough roads). In times of famine these trucks range the roads picking up cheap labour for the cities. Some are taken to the fetid slums of Salvador, others end in the rickety hovels of the mangrove swamps outside Recife, but most go to São Paulo with its swarming millions.

At first Padre Lira, besides discharging his priestly obligations, had been concerned with founding secondary schools in the small towns of the agreste. But droughts tend to run in cycles and the 'fifties were bad years, climaxing in the terrible winter of 1960.

In 1951, he was directed by Dom Inocencio, the Brazilian-born Bishop of São Raimundo, to co-ordinate famine relief in the district. This was not the hopeful task of distributing funds from abroad, but the bitter job of begging for help in his own country. In an attempt to fight official indifference he became mayor of São Raimundo, but the odds were too great.

Far into the night he wrote reports and appeals, knowing

that his efforts might be as fruitless as casting seed onto the dry earth.

And meantime, out of the caatinga stumbled the living skeletons, ragged and aimless, many of them suffering from the delusions of hunger, and he could do so little to help them. The Padre followed the miserable trail to São Paulo. Here he found the *flagelados*, the 'scourged' as the victims of the drought are called, illiterate and despised, exploited and bewildered; shacked up in slums, taking what work they could find, even on the most wretched terms.

Some of the girls became prostitutes, lost to their families, since by the archaic code of the caatinga even the brief absence together of a boy and girl would have led, at home, to a shotgun wedding.

Talking to these people the Padre found that, in spite of what they had suffered, most of them hoped to be able to scrape together the money to return home and re-stock their lands once the rain fell. Life might be hard there, but each man was his own master. Even the poorest owned a mount, if only a donkey or a mule, and each had *dignidade*. But the Padre did not underestimate the corrosive effect of city life and he knew that many would not return. He realised, too, that unless something basic could be done to change conditions of life in the caatinga this same grim pattern would be repeated with terrible monotony.

Brazilians are a kind people but do not 'strive officiously to keep alive', as Arthur Hugh Clough advised the doctors. Distances are huge and communications were poor, and until drought drove its victims into the city and despair led to riots, the plight of the under-privileged was forgotten.

A large proportion of the priests working in Brazil are foreigners but Padre Lira, being a native of the region, understood the mentality of his compatriots. He knew that his plans for the caatinga would meet with scepticism, impatience or even suspicion. Quite soberly he drew up his balance sheet.

On the debit side were the recurrent droughts; the negative

attitude of the authorities; poverty, ignorance and neglect. But on the credit side there was a healthy climate free from the endemic diseases which plague Brazil and a hardy, handsome and intelligent stock relentlessly purged by the survival only of the fittest. With their endurance, ingenuity and deep roots in the land he felt that these people could be given the means to withstand the cyclic devastation and to maintain their way of life.

But of all the people he consulted only one was ready to give encouragement. This was a kinsman, Marcos Parente, a deputy in the Brazilian parliament. Unfortunately, Marcos Parente died in September, 1958, leaving the Padre to work single-handed.

In early 1959, the Padre applied for four years' leave of absence, to go and raise funds in São Paulo.

3

THE Padre got down to São Paulo in a series of rickety buses, travelling twelve hours a day for four days to cover the 2,500 kilometres. São Paulo ranks with Tokyo as one of the fastest-growing cities in the world. They say a new building is completed every hour.

Certainly the Paulistas still have the furious energy which, not long after the city was founded in the 1600's, drove the 'Bandeirantes' out into the unexplored hinterland in search of slaves and gold and gun battles. These early pioneers have become national heroes, their ragged figures are solidified in marble and bronze, and the name 'Bandeirantes' has been used to christen avenues, squares and beaches. They symbolize the spirit of São Paulo which, with its immigrant population from all over the world, is still thrusting and tough, though the slaves are classed as free and the gold is all in the vaults.

Tired and dusty, the Padre left the coach depot and caught yet another bus to a distant suburb where the Mercedarian Fathers had their House. The Fathers were kind, but the house was full and besides this, the Padre realised that the daily bus fares into town would be too costly.

A letter from cousins in Rio was waiting for Padre Lira. They wrote that it would be difficult for a penniless priest to find accommodation in the city, and so ventured a suggestion. They were the owners of part of the Martinelli skyscraper in the centre of town. This building had a curious history. It was planned to be 340 feet high and something of a sensation, and it is still said to occupy the largest ground space of any single edifice in Brazil.

Owing to trouble with subterranean water, two companies went bankrupt before the foundations were completed. The building was carried on by a French company but before it was finished, Commendatore Martinelli's capital came to an end. He tried to sell the various floors as a number of separate condominiums, but the system was then unknown in Brazil and he found no buyers. Being a somewhat bohemian character, however, he was able to interest the promoters of a doubtful hotel and a number of dubious clubs and bars in the idea of becoming tenants.

At the request of the local immigrant colony, the Italian Government took over the building and provided the money to complete it. No respectable organisation could be persuaded to move in, and a number of women of ill repute began to squat in the vacant upper floors.

When Brazil entered the war on the side of the Allies, the Martinelli was seized by the Government and later bought at auction by the Padre's cousin, Milton, who was able to sell part of it to respectable concerns.

The Padre's relations wrote that there was an office on the twelfth floor and sleeping accommodation on the twenty-second which he was welcome to use. Their cousin must decide for himself.

The Mercedarian Fathers looked grave. The Martinelli had a terrible reputation and a priest could hardly be seen going in and out of the building. They would gladly let him stay with them if only there were another bed.

The Padre decided that the office would do nicely, but when he reached the twenty-second floor a dozen doors opened and half-naked women called and jeered. He found an empty room and lay down on the floor to sleep. Decidedly, a miracle was needed.

Next morning he left early while all the doors in the long corridors were still closed. Downstairs, the old porter shook his head. 'That floor is not for a padre,' he said, 'but I can show you an apartment on the twenty-seventh. It belongs to your cousin Milton too, but it has stood empty for twenty years, ever since Commendatore Martinelli died.'

He unlocked the door of the apartment. It was like a faded photograph. Everything lay under a thick veil of dust – panelled walls, painted ceilings, pictures in heavy frames, bathrooms tiled and mirrored. The brocade curtains hung in long grey tatters.

'This is for me,' said the Padre. The old man shook his head. 'It is madness,' he muttered.

With the spare-time help of some émigrés from São Raimundo who were employed as office cleaners, everything was soon in order. The dust clouds were so thick that some of the men fell sick, but the rest worked with a will for their countryman.

For the first few days the Padre ate in a small restaurant, but this cost too much so he bought an electric ring. Never having cooked before, he had to learn by his mistakes and was amazed to find that when he filled a saucepan with rice it swelled up and poured over the rim. However, he soon learnt to judge a panful, which he flavoured with scraps of meat or sausage, and a little chicken on Sundays. Half was eaten hot at mid-day and the other half cold in the evening. This cold evening meal lay heavy on the stomach so he started to make a soup with bread or macaroni instead. It was ten o'clock at night before he reached home and began to cook his supper and many a time, as he lay exhausted on the bed after a day spent tramping the streets, the soup boiled dry.

From his small office in the Martinelli the Padre looked down at the surging traffic below. Not only was he alone in the city, but he was alone in his ideas. Single-handed he planned to bring civilisation to a people for whom isolation and hardship was a way of life, and who distrusted change.

He began by giving his plan a concrete, legal form. Using a small bequest as founding capital he drew up and, on November 11th, 1958, registered the constitution of a Fundação Ruralista or Rural Centre. With the first money he collected the constitution was printed, and he now had something tangible to show. The Fundação had a juridical existence but not even a site, let alone the money with which to buy it. The Padre's leave of absence had been on a sink-or-swim basis and he must first find the cash for his next meal.

Through the kind offices of Padre Garcez, the chaplain, he earned small fees by celebrating mass in the church of Nossa Senhora do Rosario, five minutes from his home.

In those days small pennants carrying advertisements, slogans or gaily-coloured designs were very popular in Brazil. By selling these from door to door in offices, clubs and churches he was usually able to pay for his food and bus fares, but until the local shops came to know the 'Padre of the Martinelli' and give him credit on lean days, there were many times when he went hungry. Once, in the early stages, when an attack of 'flu confined him to bed, he lived for a week on water and sugar, the only nourishment in the flat.

Through Padre Garcez, he was appointed chaplain to the Condesa Matarazzo, wife of the descendant of an Italian immigrant of the late nineteenth century. The Matarazzos now own a shipping company, a bank, factories, farms and oil refineries. Each day the Padre went at eight o'clock to celebrate mass in the mansion on the Avenida Paulista.

For the rest of the day he tramped the streets and climbed stairs selling pennants, which he designed and printed himself on a silk screen. When, late at night, he returned home, the lift man made a preliminary trip to the upper floors.

'The Padre's coming, girls,' he would shout. 'And believe it or not,' wrote the Padre, 'I never again saw or heard anything untoward during the whole of my four years in the building, though the sight of my cassock going in at all hours did raise a scandal, and was even reported in the press.'

Having taken the Padre under their wing, the employees of the Martinelli were determined that strict discipline should be maintained and any strange woman asking to see him had to produce a satisfactory identification. A former pupil from Remanso was refused entry as her skirt was rather skimpy, and a respectable married woman who had volunteered to help in packing parcels when her office work was done also got short shrift. One evening, having worked until ten without anything to eat since lunch, she ventured downstairs to buy a sandwich. Next day, the lift man enquired of the Padre whether it was true that he had been alone with a woman behind closed doors the previous night. Explanations were of no avail. The woman was told not to return, and the Padre had to struggle with the parcels on his own.

This high moral tone had its advantages at times. A niece of the Padre's who was staying for a few days was accosted by an habitué of a shady club on the ground floor. 'Leave her alone,' said a friend, 'she's the niece of our Padre.'

Begging in São Paulo is not an easy task. People are in a hurry. In Rio they give easily but very little – a few coins to everyone who asks, and there is no unpleasantness. But the Paulista takes time to make up his mind, and time is precious. When he is convinced, he gives generously.

The Padre decided to visit factories and see if he could obtain promises of money or equipment for his Fundação. It was hard to reach the boss. There were so many minor employees anxious to shrug him off before he reached the top, and begging was painful to his pride. When he did succeed in talking to an industrialist, his project usually aroused interest. Attempting the impossible was something which appealed to a Paulista and, in any case, from a desk in São Paulo the project appeared more feasible than from the fringe of the caatinga.

To those who were interested, the Padre explained his ideas. The *catingueiros* must be brought out of their mental and physical isolation. A simple literacy programme would not be enough. As things were at present there was nothing for them to read and no need to write. The three R's would equip the people for a better life but would not provide it. At worst, the instruction would be quickly forgotten, and at best it would only encourage a flight to the towns.

The Padre saw his Fundação as a focus round which would develop rural nuclei, each with a school, and all would eventually function as community centres to which the people would contribute and from which they would benefit. The centres would offer advice and serve to disseminate new ideas.

During and immediately after their school years, pupils of both sexes would learn a skill with which they could earn money. Instead of embarking on married life with nothing more than a hut built with their own hands, some rudimentary furniture, a hammock or, if they were lucky, a bed made of staves without a mattress, they would have money put by for a few simple comforts and as a hedge against starvation should drought cause the crops to fail.

As the second stage of his plan, the Padre envisaged the formation of small communities of young married people trained in the schools to understand communal effort.

The final goal was the formation of co-operatives. It would be useless to try and impose these on people accustomed to live in isolation, but as former pupils set up homes of their own, co-operatives of an enduring nature could be formed quite naturally. Gradually money and promises of help for the project mounted up.

After a year as chaplain to the Matarazzos the Padre found

that he was attaching too much importance to the daily spell in the comfortable house, and the easily-earned money. If this went on, he might get soft. Regretfully he told the Condesa that he must give up his duties. She urged him to continue but he remained firm. The connection with the Matarazzo family, happily, was not broken, and they still supply the Fundação with materials at factory prices.

Padre Garcez came once more to the Padre's aid and got him a daily mass in the church of Iteraba in the parish of Ò. Here he helped with confessions on Saturdays and with the celebration of the major feasts of the Church and it was here that he met two nuns of the Filippini order. This casual meeting was to prove of great importance.

Many days were spent by the Padre in the districts where the flagelados, or victims of the drought who had emigrated from the North-East, tended to settle. Constantly questioning, he drew up statistics.

'How long have you been in São Paulo?'

'Would you rather remain here or return home?'

'If you would like to return home, why don't you?'

He found that families who had been in São Paulo for more than five years were, on the whole, content to remain, whereas of those recently emigrated, 90% would like to return home, but lacked the means to do so.

The apartment in the Martinelli had now become a centre for the *Piauienses* in São Paulo, above all for the humbler ones, who flocked at week-end to the twenty-seventh floor. The sale of pennants was not bringing in enough money to cover the hospitality so freely offered to his countrymen and contributions to the Fundação must remain inviolate. With the help of friends, the Padre set up a small dark-room and undertook photographic work to order.

1962, the last year of the Padre's stay in São Paulo, in spite of the gruelling routine and the snubs endured, was more pleasant. An aunt from Goiás came for six months, and one of his sisters and a niece made a protracted visit so, at the end of a long day's work, there were some of the comforts of home.

'The four years at the Martinelli,' wrote the Padre ten years later, 'are a happy memory though there were bitter moments. Because I have known hunger, I know what hunger means.'

4

AMONGST his relations in Rio the Padre had an uncle called Alcibiades, retired after a lifetime as a civil servant. Old Alcibiades had recently lost his wife and found retirement lonely, so he decided to help his favourite nephew.

'Go to the caatinga,' wrote the Padre, 'and ride through the country around Curral Novo,' a hamlet of about ten houses in the most desolate area. 'See if you can find a piece of land for sale. I now have sufficient money to pay.'

So Alcibiades travelled to Petrolina on the north-west bank of the great São Francisco River and bought a little house, taking his possessions with him. From there, he made expeditions on horseback through the mato, or scrub country. There are no absentee landlords, and families cling to the ground which they own. Land is sub-divided as sons marry, but gathered together again as the fathers die or families leave. But even close relations seldom build near one another, and houses are generally a couple of miles apart, or more.

Time passed and Alcibiades found nothing. Travel in the long rainless months is simple: dried meat, cheese and coffee in the saddle-bags, a drink of milk or a bowl of black beans where they are offered. The clean dry air is free of biting insects and at night the hammock comes out of the saddle-bags and is slung between two trees. No weary business of booking accommodation. Nothing to pay either.

At last Alcibiades wrote that he had found a woman, living

alone in a tiny hut with her goats. She was willing to sell her land at a moderate price.

The place was in the middle of nowhere. It had no name. 'Ride for an hour along the trail from Curral Novo in the direction of Oitizeiro and you will come to the land,' he wrote. 'The scrub is not cleared. There is a riacho about ten minutes away.'

'Buy it,' wired the Padre.

With some of the money he had collected in São Paulo the Padre bought a truck. This he planned to load with medicines and school equipment, furniture, crockery, linen and the sixty-six sewing-machines which he had been given. The relations in Rio had invited him to take from the twenty-seventh floor of the Martinelli anything which could be of use. Little of the furniture was suitable, but he chose a number of tables, chairs, cupboards and so on, mostly from the servants' quarters, as well as a metal filing cabinet. In the end, the truck had to make three journeys in order to carry all the material from São Paulo to Piauí.

Before the first trip could be made, however, it was necessary to hack forty-eight kilometres of road out of the mato in order to reach Curral Novo from the communal highway which runs between Petrolina and the town of Remanso. After this, there was another nine kilometres to the Fundação.

For six months Uncle Alcibiades lived and slept in the shadow of an ancient *umbuzeiro* tree not far from the old woman's hut. His hammock was tied beneath the boughs, saddle-bags slung beside it, and his small skewbald horse shared the same circle of grateful shade. Each morning he would ride out to where the hired gangs were at work. It was cruel labour under the blazing sun. Only the toughest vegetation can survive in the caatinga. Once the brief revival which follows the rains has passed foliage turns to silvery parchment or dusty grey. Twisted stems and branches are iron-hard. Cruel thorns tear the clothing. Some of the thorns are poisonous, like those of the *favela* or vulture nettle, whose whitish milk gives an agonising sting and causes fever. The ground too, with its glinting fractured stones and ribs of rock, is merciless, and everywhere there is cactus: the tall slender *facheiro* or candelabra cactus, the *mandacarú*, grotesquely branching, the *xique-xique*, its fat five-sided arms bristling with needle-sharp spikes, and the prickly pear with its thorny pads. Against this formidable armoury the men of the caatinga were prepared to pit their mattocks and machetes and the sentient whipcord of their muscles.

Under the supervision of Alcibiades the road crept on. It was rough, but it was a miracle, opening the solitary mato to the passage of a wheeled vehicle.

Meanwhile, building materials were being collected. An old manually-operated machine for making mud bricks arrived on mule-back from São Raimundo. Hand-pressed Roman tiles were drying in the sun. Strings of donkeys with lime in their panniers wound in along the trail from Sal. From the mato came bundles of facheiro stems, stripped of their thorns and split, ready to be used as rafters. Once the road was finished, timber for shutters, doors and roof beams could be brought in by truck; floor tiles and window frames floated down the São Francisco from Pirapora, where building materials were cheaper, to be picked up in Petrolina. Since there was no electricity and at first there would be no plumbing, building problems were immensely simplified.

After his long day in the saddle, Alcibiades turned in to his hammock early, but sometimes, by the light of a lamp, he would unroll the plans of the Fundação and think of the buildings which were to rise between the pegs on the great rectangle of ground which had been cleared.

The central building, with a verandah running along the whole of its front, was to house two classrooms, a work-room for machine embroidery, an office and a store. In the centre, shaded by the long roof, was an open space which would accommodate hand embroidery classes for the smaller girls.

On the left, set at right angles, there was to be a residential building. Opposite this, and forming the third side of the square, the Padre planned a hall, three sides open to the air and one end closed by a stage with a changing-room behind. This would be used for community activities. Next to the hall would stand a smaller building with one room for guests, one for the Padre, and one which would serve as a temporary chapel.

In a temperate climate houses must be secured against damp, but when the rains are of brief duration, all sorts of complications can be avoided. Near the equator, heating is no problem, though nights can be chilly. Houses built in the local style are single-storied and without ceilings. This gives extra ventilation and reveals the lovely geometry of rafters and roof tiles.

One evening, Alcibiades caught a glimpse of a dark figure loping through the brush. No man would arrive unmounted, and the stillness had not been broken by the sound of a horse's hooves. He continued quietly to eat his supper, thinking that it must have been some animal. The fire had burnt low but a branch, partly consumed, tumbled and sent up a tongue of flame.

A man was crouching in the shadows, his eyes fixed on the bowl of soup with the intent stare of a hungry dog. Alcibiades held out the bowl. The man shrank away. 'Take it,' said Alcibiades. Ignoring the spoon, the man gulped down the soup. His rangy limbs threw long shadows like a man on stilts.

'What is your name?' asked Alcibiades.

'Miguel.'

'Where do you live?'

'Nowhere.' The reply came quite naturally.

'Well, what do you do?'

'I round up stray cattle.'

'But where is your horse?'

'I have no horse.'

In a land where every man is mounted, and always clad for riding the brush in an armour of leather, this was the ultimate in destitution. Miguel's body was scarcely covered by the faded cotton shirt and trousers, ripped like his dusty skin by the cruel thickets, but he could lope like a hound through the mato and, at the end of a long day's work, he was accustomed to share the scraps of food thrown to the animals.

As Alcibiades lay in his hammock, Miguel crouched on the earth beside him, the soup glowing in his belly.

5

BY January 1963 the road to the outside world was finished and the Padre arrived with the first truckful of supplies from São Paulo. All the house staff from the Martinelli and those Piauienses who could leave their work had helped to load it. If the girls from the twenty-second floor felt any regret at the Padre's going, they had the tact not to join in the farewell.

Sufficient money to finish the Fundação building, all collected during the years in São Paulo, was deposited at a bank in Juazeiro. In the middle of the building site the flag of São Paulo was hoisted on a long pole. The Bandeirantes were giving something back to the wilderness.

The Padre hung his hammock and tethered his horse beneath his Uncle Alcibiades' tree. At the other end of the clearing stood an *umburana*, forming a dense shady umbrella. Here he set up his field altar and celebrated the first mass, the men standing round bare-headed and uncertain.

'This tree,' said Alcibiades solemnly, 'is historical.'

Day after day under the burning sun the work went on. Another load of supplies arrived from São Paulo. The timber was brought from the river port at Petrolina. During the day the Padre rode around the country visiting the isolated families. Sometimes he was away for days at a time travelling to a distant hamlet, saying mass in a ruined chapel or at points along the way, and trying to explain, in the limited time at his disposal, some of his plans for the future. Constantly he inspected the building work and checked progress against the drawings.

Each night, as the sun set, smoke rose from the mato where the men were cooking their evening gruel. The pale circle on the ground by the umbuzeiro tree slowly spread with the ash of many fires.

At the end of the week the men were paid off and rode away down the trails in the gathering darkness. While Alcibiades sat in silence smoking, with Miguel at his feet, the Padre thought over his plans.

Rural populations are usually drawn irresistibly to the cities, but most of the inhabitants of the caatinga wished to stay on their land if life could be made secure for them. This was the ultimate goal – to provide a better life by developing the potential of the people and the environment.

Various governments had embarked on schemes for rural education. Under President Dutra in the late 'forties numbers of primitive schools had been built in isolated regions, indeed there were two in the Padre's 'parish', one at Curral Novo, now used to shelter goats, and another at Moreira, fifty-two kilometres away, empty and in ruins. Even in their attempts to introduce a simple literacy programme for rural areas successive governments had met with defeat.

The first stumbling block was the lack of teachers. It was no use passing a law that a certificated teacher, before obtaining a post in a town, must work for at least a year in a rural zone. Young girls were naturally unwilling to go to lonely spots where they would have to share the miserable food and accommodation of the inhabitants and go without any form of amusement or civilised company. Places without electric light or sufficient water and without any means of transport to their homes but horseback, or an occasional truck. So the law had an escape clause. If enough trained teachers could not be found, then 'lay' teachers would be accepted. But even such semi-literate girls were hard to recruit since their pay, in the State of Piauí, was only from £1.50 to £2 a month and they were expected to cope with classes averaging sixty children, often in buildings devoid of any equipment.

In despair, the government proposed a programme of education by radio or television, but in backward rural areas there was no money to pay for apparatus and rarely any electric current.

In the Padre's 'parish' the population averaged one person per square kilometre. In Curral Novo, the official centre of the area, there were only twenty families within a radius of three kilometres, and at the same distance from the Fundação, not more than seven. If, in such an unfavourable situation, the Padre could organise a programme of education, this should serve as an encouragement to the rest of the backward areas of Brazil.

One morning a man came riding in from Cacimbas, a small hamlet thirty kilometres away. Could the Padre come at once, his small daughter had been bitten by a snake.

'I have serum,' said the Padre, 'but many hours will have passed.'

'We have rubbed salt into the wound,' said the man eagerly. This was the traditional remedy. They set out at once.

The new road would take them to Curral Novo, but after that there were twenty more kilometres of rough track which would slow their pace.

'The cat attacked a snake. It killed the cat and then came into the house where the children were sleeping on the floor and bit Doralda in the throat. She is very bad.'

So there was hope. Salt would do no good, but some of the venom must have been spent in the battle with the cat.

The child lived, though for many weeks she was half blind and found great difficulty in swallowing. The Padre sensed a lessening of resistance in the local parents. For, as he had expected, his talk of opening schools had been met everywhere with a total lack of enthusiasm, if not mistrust.

Children, even when quite small, were regarded as the natural slaves of their fathers and continued to be until they married and set up homes of their own. The years before the children were born and those after the last of them left home were the lean years for the parents, with no free labour on which to draw. It would, of course, be convenient for a man to have someone in the family who could sign a document or read a simple form, but this would not outweigh the burden of keeping a child decently clothed or compensate for the loss of his labour. Decidedly schools were a threat.

There were only ten primitive houses in the hamlet of Cacimbas though settled along the neighbouring shallow valley there were forty-one families with two hundred and twenty members. Had land been for sale, this would have provided a more favourable site for the Fundação, especially since, during the drought of 1951, when even the bitter water beneath the sand of the riachos had dried up, a natural rock basin had been discovered only a few kilometres away. An old man had wandered in with the story of a great rock lying beneath the surface in a spot where plants remained green all through the summer. Scraping away the sand they had discovered a natural cistern, which held the winter rains. This could be enlarged and dammed to form a reservoir of some capacity.

The dilapidated chapel of Cacimbas could be repaired at a reasonable cost and used, in the early stages, as a school. Here, at least, was the basis of a rural nucleus.

These ideas were practical and modest, but the Padre was clear-sighted enough to realise that they contained an element of wishful thinking. As a native of Piauí, he could appreciate the strength of the forces arrayed against him: poverty, ignorance, apathy and mistrust. Even the children who had joined the classes of the two abortive State schools had preferred hard labour at home to the constraint and boredom, and this was not forgotten. Every difficulty stood out as clearly as each dry leaf in the incandescent light of day, or each small rustle and cry in the immense silence of the night.

Gradually, the Padre's plans were crystallising. The local way of life could not be altered to suit his plans, but these must be adapted to local conditions. Instead of the usual two school terms a year, he would introduce one term, lasting from May 1st to November 30th. In this way, the children would be at home to help their fathers during the sowing and harvesting which took place in the rainy season. They could also remain at home in safety when the rains turned the riachos into dangerous torrents.

To solve the clothing difficulty, he would provide a uniform for each child, a black cotton skirt or trousers and a pale blue shirt with the badge of the Fundação – a white flower on a barren branch – embroidered on the pocket. Each child would receive a pair of shoes to be worn in school hours in place of their rough everyday sandals.

The Padre distrusted paternalism and felt that all his pupils should eventually repay what they had received. He felt strongly, too, that the Fundação must become self-supporting as soon as possible.

The women of North-East Brazil have shown a marked talent for embroidery. Usually their work is exploited, being bought up at sweated-labour rates. With his connections in São Paulo, the Padre felt sure of a market and he planned to lay in supplies of raw materials once a year and, at the same time, to sell the year's stock of finished embroidery. More frequent journeys would be too expensive. Each pupil would be credited with a fair rate for her work, but this would not be paid until she was married or independent, otherwise the money would simply be confiscated by her father. On leaving school, each girl would have the right to buy a sewing-machine at cost price with which she could continue working at home. The average monthly earning for a girl would be as high as the State minimum wage for a man. Very few of the men in the area earned anything at all, being accustomed to live by barter, so that the capacity to earn money would rapidly change the debased status of the women.

But this change of status would threaten to introduce an imbalance in the younger generation, and a skill must be found for the boys. In the whole of South-East Piauí there was no shoe factory and the demand for rough shoes and sandals was great since, with the sharp stones and poisonous snakes of the caatinga, not even the poorest could go unshod.

Once the shoe factory could be set up and made to function, it would in some ways be a better proposition than the embroidery classes, since hides could be obtained in Juazeiro and the finished product sold locally.

Like a man walking a tight rope who keeps his eyes fixed on a steady point ahead, because if he looks at what is below him he will fall, the Padre forced himself not to brood on the obstacles in his way.

It was in May 1964 that the sister of one of the nuns whom the Padre had met in São Paulo, herself a nun in the Filippini Convent in Winchester, happened to meet a widow who was interested in pioneer work. Sister Mary talked about the priest who was planning to bring new life to a desolate area in North-East Brazil and of the lonely and discouraging task which he faced.

During the war, Muriel Heading Mitchell had lost her husband, a volunteer naval chaplain who went down in the cruiser *Charybdis*. Both her children had settled in the New World, so she knew what loneliness meant.

She asked Sister Mary for the address of the Padre and pored over an atlas without being able to find the place where he was working. Muriel decided to write to the Padre in Spanish, since she did not speak Portuguese, hoping that he would understand. Her own life in recent years had been a struggle, both with illness and the problem of making ends meet on a meagre service pension, and she felt deeply drawn to this lonely man.

With the help of friends she collected a boxful of used clothes, toys and simple medicines and sent them off. The chances that these and the letter she had posted in the pillar box at the corner of Teg Down Meads would ever reach a nameless spot in the Brazilian backlands seemed more than remote. Months passed and there was no reply.

Meanwhile, a spearhead of opposition to the Padre was forming around Seu José, the owner of the one small shop in Curral Novo (Seu is the colloquial shortening for Senhor). For years, Seu José had exchanged goatskins, the only thing the people could sell, for simple necessities like salt, sugar and coffee. He priced the commodities high, but paid only half the going rate for the skins. For the locals there was no option. He had cornered the market. Now, however, the Fundação truck took the skins to Petrolina, where they sold for double, and brought back goods at market prices. It was obvious that if business was to continue as before, the Padre must be made to leave the area.

Rumours began to spread. This Padre was up to no good. Why did he want to get hold of all the little girls? What was all this religion about? Where did he get his money? What had he been doing in the city all these years? The people of the caatinga were not naturally responsive, but this smear campaign certainly made things more difficult.

A stranger might have been tempted to give up, but Padre Lira was prepared to be patient. In one of his first reports he wrote, 'The indifference of these people and their apathy are some of the greatest obstacles to progress. They don't react and they don't argue. When invited to a meeting they come promptly, listen attentively to what is said and when asked to give their opinion, agree with everything. But they leave thinking and acting exactly as before.

'Born and brought up in a region which is totally abandoned by the outside world, in surroundings where nature itself, with its stony soil, gnarled trees, rending thorns, bitter water, recurrent droughts and stifling heat is the embodiment of uffering, these men are cowed and beaten. Their slow droning voices are an echo of the desolation which lies within them.

'Rather than indifferent, they are mistrustful. They believe in no one and hope for nothing. Recognition of their own social insignificance has bred such a profound sense of inferiority that even those who try to help are regarded as intruders who merely upset their way of life. Thcy suspect that school is a ruse to deprive them of their children's labour. "A blind beggar distrusts too large a gift," they say.

'Far from being bad, these men are honest and would never willingly hurt anyone. But isolation is in their blood. It is like a canker. This urge for solitude shows even in the way that close relatives will build their houses far apart. These people have been branded as indolent. This is not true. They have always existed on the fringe, but with guidance and help their excellent qualities can be developed.'

In the spring, the Padre's morale was lifted by a visit to São Paulo. His old friends at the Martinelli greeted him with delight and flocked to offer him old clothes, medicines and all sorts of contributions for the Fundação. Even the prostitutes came with small offerings for the poor in Piauí.

In the apartment on the twenty-seventh floor the Padre organised a *feijoada*, the traditional Brazilian meal of black beans, meat and sausage in a gravy rich with onions, herbs, garlic and tomatoes, served with manioc flour fried in butter, sliced orange, shredded dark-green cabbage and rice. Every single employee of the Martinelli was there with husband or wife, though some had to take their turn to eat while a colleague replaced them on duty.

'It was a charming occasion,' the Padre later told us, 'we had to eat very slowly so that everyone felt included in the banquet, and just towards the end there was a cry, "We can't finish until Nelson has arrived." Somehow the man who minded the boiler had been overlooked, and he appeared, very flustered, to a round of clapping. They were all simple people, but they made the most delightful speeches.'

Ten months after Muriel's parcel had been posted, a letter smudgily typed on what looked like large sheets of old fashioned lavatory paper, arrived in Winchester. It was dated March 8th, 1965.

'*Estimada Senhora,*' it began, 'I cannot describe my joy and astonishment when I received a letter from abroad and I must confess that I was greatly moved. The world is very small, I thought. How can it be that someone as far away as England can know that we exist in these empty lands? Since this is the first time that I write, perhaps the Senhora will excuse the length of my letter as I have so much to tell.'

He went on to describe the country and conditions and the problems which he faced, the lack of communications and the long hours in the saddle.

'Besides being a waste of time, these journeys are hard on one's health. I am not so young, [At this time he was only forty-three, but as a man of the North-East he was very much aware of the brevity of life] and I have had trouble with a stomach ulcer and a throat complaint.

'The Bishop of São Raimundo wants to make this into an official parish next year so I am working on the reconstruction of the chapel of Curral Novo which was in ruins when I arrived in January, 1963. The roof is partly repaired and now we are going to restore the altar and do up the inside of the building. Unfortunately, we have nothing for the altar but my travelling mass kit.

'I could go on writing all night, but I will wait until the next letter to tell you more. Mail has to be taken once a month to Juazeiro and letters are collected from our post box there, so one must put up with delays.'

6

EVERYTHING was now ready at the Fundação and the Padre invited children between the ages of seven and fourteen to register. He had devised a form which he would help each parent to complete. This form would give precise information about every family and its members, living or dead, besides the type of house they lived in, their land, water supply, herds and crops, and their standard of literacy. In time, these forms would provide the basis for a social survey of the region, as well as a guide for the distribution of medical aid, or for relief during a period of drought.

Six young teachers, courteously referred to as 'professoras', had been recruited in the small towns of the agreste and term was due to start in a few weeks, but only a handful of pupils had registered. School opening at the Fundação was postponed for a month. Cacimbas was the one place which showed any enthusiasm and a benefactress in São Paulo offered to pay a teacher if a school could be set up there.

To make up the necessary numbers, the Padre announced that adults up to thirty could come for one year and learn to read and write. On June 1st, 1965, the Fundação school opened with seventy-two pupils of various ages. At the same time, forty children joined the school at Cacimbas.

In July, Muriel heard from the Padre once more. 'Your letter of April 7th reached me on June 20th. I will try to answer your questions. There are six outlying chapels in the "parish". Two of them are near the Fundação at 18 and 30 kilometres distance. The rest are between 60 and 120 kilometres away. All of them are small and dilapidated and none holds more than a hundred people, so that the faithful must attend in turn. These people are Catholic by tradition, but they have no idea of the mysteries of the Faith and confuse religion with superstitious practices which are very hard to eradicate. Progress will be slow.

'Your suggestion that Oxfam might help to get transport for me seems like a dream. I have heard of them. They have done wonderful things . . .'

At the beginning of September the Padre wrote again. The first term had not been easy. The children were mostly undernourished. Used to living in solitude and seeing only their own families, they were bewildered and silent and had no idea how to play. The only activity which they performed readily was eating. The parents on the other hand, that is to say the fathers, since the mothers' opinion was of no account, were disappointed that the pupils did not immediately learn to read and write. What use were their sacrifices if the children couldn't even read the Padre's form? True, they had put on a little weight, but still not all of them could write their father's name correctly.

'I want school to be so much more than just a simple experiment in literacy. I want school to give the children everything that they lack in their homes – human warmth, recreation, comfort, music, even food. I want it to be a real home for them.

'The news that you are sending money for altar furnishings is immensely encouraging,' wrote the Padre, 'and I thank you from my heart. It is sad to think that though we have a children's playground equipped with swings and seesaws given us by a benefactor in São Paulo, we have as yet no proper chapel. Since the money collected for the Fundação was given for a specific purpose, I cannot use it for the chapels, but when I have gained the confidence of the people here, this work will be done. A church should be built by the people who use it, poor though they may be. I am making a collection, not in cash, since this seldom changes hands, but of livestock. Those who can afford it will give an ox or a cow, others a sheep, goat or pig, or perhaps a hen or a few eggs. These I can exchange for labour or building materials. When the people heard of your gift they were delighted. "Now things are really moving," they said.

'I have been to Brasilia to apply for a grant for the Fundação. [This had been allocated in 1964 by his cousin, Joaquim Parente, who was a senator, but official application had to be made each year.]

'Everything connected with official business here in Brazil is so painfully slow that a person who is not naturally patient would be forced to despair, but your letter filled me with hope. It is always like this. When the Devil closes a window, God opens a door.

'You ask me what happens if anyone is ill. There is no doctor here but me, not even a *curandeiro* (folk healer). On the whole, health is good, though. We are free from malaria, and our worst disease is hunger. The nearest pharmacy is 120 kilometres away. If someone falls ill they either lie down and die or, if they can afford it – and very few can – they send for medicines from São Raimundo [a two-day journey on horseback each way] or for a doctor who must come by hired jeep.

'When I first came here I started to record every death in my "parish" and discovered what a high proportion of mothers died as a result of giving birth. My friends in Rio and São Paulo were shocked at the figures and even I, born in the region and working all my life in the prelacy, had not been aware of the extent of the deaths.'

Strangely enough, St Raymond Nonnatus, after whom São Raimundo is called, is the patron saint of midwives and owes his curious name, 'the unborn' to having been taken from his mother's womb after her death.

'You ask, too, if the Papal Nuncio knows of our needs. He knows nothing about this region – only about the general problems of the North-East.

'Our prelacy is the only area in Brazil served entirely by native-born priests, and this thanks to the late Dom Inocencio who devoted his life to training them. Dom Amadeo the present bishop, who is a Spaniard, tells us that his total income from the prelacy last year amounted to only £40 and but for the help of Propaganda Fide he would have gone hungry.

'The situation all over the eastern part of the prelacy is the same, except that the official parishes possess some centre, town or village.

'I believe more and more that a school is the only way of bringing people together. I must repeat that the people are good, of a captivating simplicity, but they need guidance and care. The material help which the Senhora is giving us is of great value, but the feeling of solidarity with people in England also brings real human comfort to the catingueiros.'

In the second letter the Padre warned Muriel, 'Your plans to send small comforts are touching, but I am afraid I must warn you that the postal services in this part of Brazil do not deserve confidence. All packages are opened and the best items usually removed. I know of endless cases, and so I advise you to send things by freight or not at all. It will be wonderful if the Christmas presents you have chosen for the children really arrive.

'After four or five months of apprenticeship the girls are producing embroidery of real artistic value. Now we must organise the trade for the boys. I feel certain that when the results of our work become known some group will be prepared to assist us, not by doling out charity, but by helping us to gain our independence.

'This year we have been obliged to close the school early through lack of water. We had to bring it a distance of 18 kilometres on mule-back. Now this source has dried up. If God withholds the rains we shall face terrible problems. The Senhora cannot imagine what this means. We have had ten good winters with abundant rain but before this, we had ten bad ones. Drought is a constant spectre and we must somehow see that people's lives don't depend on something so uncertain as the seasonal rains.

'The problem of drinking water, at least, could be solved if we could build cisterns to catch the rainwater which runs from the roofs, but we haven't the money. Cement is so expensive, almost £2 a sack. A better solution is to build reservoirs but, apart from the outlay, this requires a technician. The cheapest method is to scrape out natural rock basins like the one at Cacimbas, but the only suitable places are a long way from the Fundação and the water would have to be carried on donkey-back. In term time there are over a hundred people at the Fundação who require drinking water every day.

'I am starting the desobriga. The thought of riding is even more wearisome now that I have the prospect of other transport. How quickly one becomes spoilt! This is the worst time of the year for travelling. The heat builds up in a long crescendo until the rains, which normally start in November. As a priest, I must not neglect my spiritual duties, but I have not the Christian resignation to endure with patience the long wasted hours on horseback. At this season of the year, nature is dead. Except for the juazeiro, the trees are leafless. One can travel for days without finding a single patch of shade.

'You ask if there are mountains here. The country is rolling and even the hills which divide the States of Piauí and Bahia are low and form no more than a symbolical boundary. There are no forests either, just the caatinga of the North-East with twisted, stunted trees, sparse and ugly.

'You say my life is hard. I can reply with absolute sincerity that as I grow older I feel more fulfilled than ever before. As we began here with nothing, every trifle means so much, quite different from working in a big city where the results of one's efforts do not show. It is true that one should do good for its own sake, but it is wonderful to have found work which is so rewarding.'

7

MURIEL was determined that the Padre should have a jeep. She began by writing a letter to the *Catholic Herald*, asking for public support. Her letter was heavily blue-pencilled and the result, only ten shillings.

She made an approach to Oxfam, but they, believing the Padre's work to be of a purely missionary nature, replied that they could only support social welfare developments and relief programmes. Muriel is a comely woman who carries her age gracefully. Her motherly appearance can prove very deceptive and under the apple blossom skin there is a firm and even pugnacious jaw.

She returned to the attack, writing also to CRS (Catholic Relief Services) in Rio, asking if they would forward parcels to Padre Lira. They replied that this would be too expensive and troublesome.

In September 1965, the *Catholic Herald* carried a leader on the Church and poverty. Muriel wrote to the editor describing the rebuffs she had suffered. Her letter was published in full and attracted contributions of over £200, the first being £5 from 'an Irish Catholic in London' with the helpful suggestion that 'CRS ought to be shot'.

Muriel now wrote to the Publicity Officer of Oxfam, whose attention had already been drawn to her second letter in the *Catholic Herald*, correcting the misapprehension about the Padre's work and saying that as she now had £215, would Oxfam give the other £500 necessary to buy a jeep for Padre Lira. This was approved, to Muriel's delight.

After this, there was a long silence and then a letter arrived headed 'Rio, December 12th, 1965'. It brought disquieting news.

'I have been here since the 15th November and have been very ill,' wrote the Padre, 'but thank God, the danger has passed and I left hospital three days ago feeling almost myself, though very weak.

'The desobriga began on October 25th. The heat was horrible and many visits had to be cancelled for lack of water. Five days before the end of the journey I began to feel ill – high fever, vomiting, stomach pains and so on. I tried to continue the journey but it was impossible. Fortunately I was only ten leagues [about 40 miles] from home as the crow flies. There was no alternative but to return. They wanted to carry me in a hammock. They tie the hammock to a pole which two men carry on their shoulders. This is the usual way of transporting sick people, or bodies for burial if the cemetery is distant.

'I was unable to ride, but I couldn't be brought to the Fundação in a hammock. Everyone would have thought I was dying and the emotional strain would have been too much! I rested for a whole day in a hovel and prayed to Nossa Senhora das Mercês. Next day I attempted the journey on horseback, starting very early in the morning. The first few hours were a misery, but then the vomiting diminished – it was that which worried me most – and I was able to continue. I took three days to cover the sixty kilometres, travelling by night and in the early morning. The good little professoras had heard the news and sent for a doctor, hoping that he could go out to meet me, but both the doctors in São Raimundo were away answering calls in the *sertão*, as we call the wilderness. An hour or two after I reached the Fundação one of them was there and spent three days at my bedside. He said that I must have really thorough treatment.

'Arriving here in Rio, I was met by friends and relations at the airport and taken straight to hospital. Diagnosis: severe amoebic infection, aggravation of the stomach ulcer and goodness knows what else.

'Although I am so poor, I lacked for nothing. The excellent

doctor charged no fees and the hospital and even the laboratory tests and X-rays were free. Only the medicines had to be paid for. I lost twelve kilos and am down to fifty-three [eight stone five].

'I don't know how to thank God for so much goodness. And to crown all these consolations, I received your letter. My sister, to whom I showed it, says I have found a mother. I lost my mother and father when I was seven years old.

'Forgive me if this long letter bores you, but I am depressed and sick, far from my own Piauí, and I gain such real pleasure from talking to you that I never feel weary. From time to time I stop, smoke a cigarette, and then continue. I wonder if you would like a Portuguese dictionary. Tell me honestly. It would be easy for me to find one in Rio.

'The doctor has forbidden me to do any tiring work here in the South. Pray that I may regain my strength rapidly because, as I told the doctor, my life without work is meaningless. And as for living on others, rather than that, I pray God will take me to my rest.

'I shall stay here until the 22nd and then go to spend Christmas quietly in a home for old folks run by the Spanish Little Sisters of the Poor who were so good to me during the difficult years in São Paulo. I am sad at not being able to spend Christmas with my dear children. They were radiant when they heard that a parcel would be arriving from you.'

News of the jeep had meanwhile reached the Padre and two days before Christmas he wrote of his delight. 'In spite of what you tell me I cannot believe it. For me it is a dream. To possess a jeep and travel in comfort. What a wonderful Christmas present! *Como Deus é bom*! Now everything will be so much easier.

'I was disappointed that the doctor forbade me to go to São Paulo where so much has to be done, but there was a consolation. When I went to see Father Leising at CRS, he told me that orders to buy a jeep had reached him, but that it would not be ready until February or March. It is a pity you don't understand our slang. See if someone can translate this for you. Father Leising said to me, "The Senhora is *muito chata* [very importunate] but she's a woman of spirit. You have a real friend in England.' "

8

THERE were obviously some forces, like the Brazilian postal services, which Muriel could not overcome. She decided that her next target must be the vocational training for the boys at the Fundação. With the help of her brother, Kenneth Benton, a member of the Diplomatic Service, she made an approach to Sir Hugh Ellis Rees, Administrator of the Catholic Fund for Overseas Development, and was able to tell the Padre that Cafod would be prepared to help in setting up a shoe factory.

On January 2nd, 1966, he wrote from Rio, 'All this good news, the thought that there are crates of clothes coming from you by sea, the Christmas card signed by you and all your friends and, most of all, my jeep, have helped my recovery enormously. The doctor is amazed and says that if I will put on a little weight, I can go to São Paulo after all.

'I had hoped to travel back by jeep to Piauí and we could have saved so much expense by loading it with supplies, but for some reason which I don't understand, CRS says that it cannot be delivered before February.

'The drought in Piauí is now a reality, and some families have already left the region. Those with children at school are determined to hold out in the belief that they will be fed.'

A month later the Padre wrote, 'I arrived three days ago. Once more I am in the enchanting solitude of the sertão. There is no one else here at the Fundação, but I don't feel lonely.

Even the hamlet of Curral Novo is deserted, as Providence has at last sent abundant rain and all the families, with their children, are out sowing their crops. When I arrived the scene was desolate, the animals dying of hunger and the children agonisingly thin. The professoras told me that when term ended they said, "Now we are going to suffer hard times". They long for school to start again, so different from children in other places who sigh for the holidays and are sad when they end. Thank God, though, there is drinking water at last and I have even had a bath.

'Now that I am alone I can get on with the paperwork. I have to fill in dozens of forms in the hope of getting some help from the Government. Our system is bureaucratic in the extreme and each application has to be accompanied by a mountain of documentation. I must also account for everything I have received. This quiet time can be used to make reports for Oxfam and Cafod too. I don't find it easy to write such things and am rather slow at it, especially since the doctor has forbidden me, for the present, to write by the light of a paraffin lamp, so I can only work by day.

'They say in Rio that one of the documents of the jeep is still missing and I don't know when this will arrive. I have asked my brother in Brasilia whether he can take delivery of the vehicle and bring it here, but I don't think we shall be motorised before March. Having waited so long, I suppose we can wait for one month more.

'In spite of the two trips I made to Santos from São Paulo and all the efforts of my friends, the crates of clothing could not be found. Just as I was leaving São Paulo the documents arrived, but I could not wait. A friend will try to get the crates released and send them up in the jeep.

'The parcels which you addressed to the Filippini Sisters arrived safely together with your letter. Incidentally, the nuns who, like all women, are curious, could not resist opening them and were astonished at the excellent quality of the clothes you have sent. I have finally persuaded them that, for some years at least, conditions will not be fit for them to come and work here.

'Our return journey from São Paulo was difficult because of the weather, and the truck broke down several times. We were three days on the way, and one night we slept in a forest while the rain poured down. Luckily I was able to spend the night in the driver's cab.

'It is still raining and the seed has been washed out of the ground. The whole harvest, except for a small quantity of black beans, will be lost. It is too late to sow again. The harvest here is never large. We produce no cash crops but when all goes well, enough corn, manioc and black beans to last each family for the year. At least the belated rains have brought some grazing for the animals and it is wonderful to see the caatinga fresh and green.

'There is still no news of the money you sent for the altar. This matter is now urgent as the bishop has written that he intends to visit us. A bishop has never before set foot here, so this is a big event. If we can build the 60 kilometres of road to Barra do Bonito, the most isolated of all our hamlets, and if the jeep arrives in time, I shall be able to show him the terribly primitive state of the people there.

'The previous transfer of money arrived safely. Please will you thank your kind elder brother for the share he contributed and also the Carmelite Sisters. I marvel that they can spare £5 out of their tiny resources. God forbid that I should spend £11 on one cassock! With the total of £30 I bought three cassocks, socks, shoes, toilet soap, a whole year's supply of kitchen soap, razor blades and shaving cream, as well as new lenses for my spectacles and a small present for each of the professoras.

'Your Christmas parcel is in Salvador and the post office say that I must go and fetch it – a twelve-hour journey from Juazeiro each way – so this will have to wait until I go to Salvador in April. I shall distribute the contents of the parcel at the First Communion celebrations in May, which we shall combine with Mothers' Day.

'And now I am going to ask you something which will give me great happiness. My sister was right when she said that I had found a mother in you. Will you allow me to sign this letter in the way in which I feel: "Your Brazilian son"?'

Muriel responded gladly and from then on, the Padre addressed his letter to his *mãe ingleza*, or English mother.

9

BY taking on extra teaching work, Muriel had been able to save enough to fly out and spend Christmas in California. The Padre followed the trip with interest and wrote, 'I can imagine how happy your family was to see you. Nothing is too good for a mother. I lost this happiness as a little boy and everyone says that my mother was so good and kind.

'Did I tell you how much I regret all the time you spend translating my letters with a dictionary? Writing to you is such a joy that I don't even mind if my letters are understood or not. I write as if I were talking to you. This makes me very happy, but when I receive your letters, my happiness overflows. You may not believe it, but I leave your letters on my desk and read them again and again – sometimes right through from the first, and I thank God.

'And now some worrying news. Father Leising of CRS in Rio has written that the jeep is in São Paulo ready to be fetched, but they need Cr$200 [two hundred cruzeiros] more. I replied that I would be very happy to pay but I have no money and suggested that he might pass on to me some mass stipends. He has a great many from America and spared me a few when I was in Rio.

'Still no sign of the clothing from Santos. Anyone who suffered from impatience would become a chronic invalid in Brazil.'

Muriel was not the woman to suffer delay with resignation. She had not hesitated to attack CRS about the matter of forwarding parcels. Now, she waded in with one of her sharper letters. The Senhora was certainly *chata*, but to good effect.

On March 17th, the Padre wrote, 'With boundless joy I must tell you that I received the jeep yesterday. It is beautiful, a splendid petroleum blue. My brother, knowing how I longed for it, sent his son down to São Paulo as soon as it was released. The boy had to return via Brasilia and then come on here, a journey of almost 5,000 kilometres. I shall not attempt to drive it myself as I am without any mechanical aptitude whatever, but there is a boy here who can drive. Tomorrow I am taking the jeep to São Raimundo to prepare a petition for the Ministry of Education. Now, I can name the date when I will travel and on which I shall return, not like the time when I might have to wait a month to pick up a truck.'

In his delight over the jeep, and having at last a tangible link with the outside world, the Padre missed no chance of talking about his good fortune.

'Everyone who has heard that our jeep was financed largely by Oxfam (and believe me, I do not forget the part which you and your friends played) has been astonished. People simply cannot believe that Oxfam could have heard of our work in the caatinga.

'Whilst I was in Juazeiro the other day I called on the doctor. He advised me to give up smoking, unlike the doctors in Rio and São Paulo. Even if they had done so, I should have taken no notice. I have smoked since I was a boy and I really enjoy a cigarette.

'I bought seedlings of orange, coconut and banana trees from Juazeiro. Last year we planted tomatoes, lettuce, red peppers, carrots and so on, but everything was killed by the water here which was terribly saline. I hope this season the salt content will be less. It varies from year to year.

'As the result of an application to the former Minister of

Justice, Juracy Magalhaes, who has been a good friend to us, we have received a grant of two million old cruzeiros [then about £350]. Unfortunately he has now been transferred to the Ministry of Foreign Affairs and will have no more funds at his disposal. With this money we shall be able to excavate about 500 cubic metres of earth and rock at a spot not far from the Fundação where the ground appears to be impermeable. If only it rains in April as it did last year, we should have drinking water to last until December.'

At the beginning of April the Padre wrote that there had been a recurrence of his former illness and that he had been invited by a religious order in Salvador to spend a few days with them while he visited the doctor. This was useful, since he could fetch the Christmas parcel and also post a few important letters.

On April 7th he wrote from Salvador, 'This city is full of memories for me as I was at school in the Benedictine Seminary here. At long last I was able to open your parcel. It is full of wonderful presents for the children, tiny dolls and so many things to delight them.

'The money for the altar has finally been traced. It was sent to Teresina, the capital of the State of Piauí, but no advice reached me. Our postal service is so miserably bad, in spite of a great improvement under the new government. Perhaps the crates of clothes which are stuck in Santos will turn up one day. Whoever works in Piauí must adopt the principles of our native Indians who consider that time is quite limitless.

'They say here in Salvador that the whole of the North-East is suffering from drought. All that I saw during my relief work in the 'fifties has left me with a real terror of this. It was then that I decided to dedicate my life to the people of the caatinga who are the chief victims. Drought is our inseparable companion and we must learn to live with it. People's lives must not be allowed to depend on rain, which so often fails, and we must find for them a means of earning money so that they can take steps to conserve water and buy the necessities of life when the land denies them. With our adverse climate we can never produce sufficient food in the bad years. I fear that the land, at those times, rather than feeding the people, is nourished by the bodies of those who are buried in it.

'During the bad times, food must be brought in from outside, but charity will only debase my people. I have been promised supplies of Food for Peace through Caritas Brasileira and this can be used to pay men for building the roads which we so urgently need. The wants of these people are so simple. Some corn or manioc meal and a little oil to add to their gruel will carry them through the lean months until they are able to drink their own milk and have home-made cheese and dried meat once more.

'In the meantime, each man who is working on the roads will receive an amount of food corresponding to the size of his family, and receive it proudly, having earned it with work which will open up the country and bring lasting benefit. You can imagine how delighted I was to receive this promise of food. Engineer Farias is coming on behalf of Caritas to inspect the road work we have done so far.

'We have already excavated 200 cubic metres of the new reservoir. The ground is as hard as iron and really needs dynamite. The scanty rain which fell in March evaporated immediately and there is little hope of rain after Holy Week. Last night a few clouds gathered and there was prolonged lightning, but it came to nothing. The children are so pale and thin. I had hoped to have drinking water for the coming year. If we can finish the reservoir we shall have water for other uses as well.'

In May 1966, Muriel's youngest brother, Kenneth Benton, was posted as Counsellor to the British Embassy, Rio de Janeiro. The Padre was delighted. 'Now I shall be able to send you the goatskin which has been tanned for you in São Raimundo,' he wrote, 'for I shall insist that your brother visits the Fundação. Our goatskins are the best in the country and usually they are sent to Germany for preparation and then back to Brazil to be made into luxury articles. I fear that your skin is not very expertly tanned, but it is from a large and handsome animal.

'Our First Communion was a great success. Little by little we are conquering the indifference of these people. For the first time some of the men came with their children. The mass was in dialogue and all the children responded. Afterwards we paid tribute to the mothers, an impressive innovation since most of the people had never considered that they owed their mothers anything at all.

'Our wonderful jeep has already travelled some 15,000 kilometres and taken eight sick people to São Raimundo or Juazeiro. On the 22nd of this month we expect the first visit of a doctor who will come to Curral Novo and this visit will be repeated every month. Without the jeep, this would have been impossible.

'Engineer Farias arrived three days ago and will stay for another three. He works under Father Leising in CRS and is advising us about building reservoirs. It seems that he was impressed with our road-building and he is certainly a good friend. He is our first visitor.

'Finally, the best news I have to give is that God had mercy on us and sent rain on April 12th, the day after my return from Salvador. The harvest was entirely lost, but at least we have some water to drink. Two and a half inches fell in three hours. It was a miracle.'

At the beginning of June the Padre wrote that his report for Cafod was nearly complete. It was thirty-three pages long – almost a book – but it was important that the Administration should know as much as possible about the region. The jeep was going wonderfully, though two tyres had already worn through on the stony roads.

A week later he wrote that the money for the altar had finally been received and that the delay had perhaps been a blessing, since the value of the pound had risen in relation to the cruzeiro during the ten months of waiting.

'I have just suffered an attack of malaria,' he wrote. 'This frightened me, since as a young man I nearly died of it, but medicine has advanced tremendously. I took a large dose of the remedy. The reaction was very strong, but the fever did not return.

'Yesterday I came back from São Raimundo where I saw Dom Amadeo, the Bishop, who returned from Spain a week ago. He has been Bishop of São Raimundo for five years but, owing to the Ecumenical Council and a long illness which kept him in his native country, he has very seldom been here. I had hoped that Curral Novo might be made the centre of an official parish and that the name would be changed to Dom Inocencio, but it has been demoted to the status of a simple hamlet and the name Curral Novo must remain. Dom Amadeo says that he does not wish to establish us as a canonical parish yet, though he may consider this next year. He is coming to the Fundação on September 24th, Feast of Nossa Senhora das Mercês.

'School is going well. The professoras are planning a celebration on June 23rd, Feast of St John, and they are teaching the children the quadrilha, an old-fashioned Portuguese dance which has become traditional here. It is not easy, as so many of the children have no aptitude.

'The professoras send you many messages. They are so young and gay and work very hard, even taking catechism classes all through Sunday, both at the Fundação and Cacimbas. Next month they are to have a treat. I am taking them in our precious jeep to the great new power station on the falls of the São Francisco River at Paulo Afonso. It is a trip of 300 kilometres each way over dust roads and will take five days, but the girls are enchanted. They will make up lost classes by teaching on Saturdays which are normally free days.

'We are very anxious about the drought. The brief rains

which fell at the beginning of the month were not repeated, and the sky remains as blue as the jeep. If no more rain falls it will be disastrous. But at least if we can build reservoirs there is hope for the future.'

On July 7th the Padre reported that he had collected ten tons of food sent by Caritas Brasileira to Juazeiro. Over 100 men were now working on the roads and, counting their families, about 700 people were being fed.

The cost of transporting food was very high, as well as the handling charges which had to be paid to Caritas for each load. The Padre planned to apply in Brasilia for a grant to meet this heavy expenditure.

'How happy your letters make me. My life has changed completely in the last year. Please thank your friends the Carmelite nuns for their messages. The prayers of women who live entirely dedicated to God are of more value than money. I think this is why things have gone so much better this year. The professoras are touchingly devoted; the children in the catechism classes are always enthusiastic. I have even had several calls to sick beds – a thing which never happened before.

'The day after I return from Paulo Afonso I shall continue the roadless stretches of the desobriga on horseback, taking a week. On the 20th I shall visit by jeep the chapel of Ponta da Serra, 120 kilometres from the Fundação, and go directly from there to Petrolina, where I shall take an aeroplane for Brasilia next day. From there I leave for Rio, where I hope to see your brother, and shall then go to São Paulo. I am determined to trace the missing crates of clothes.

'After completing various necessary visits round here, and the *Festas da Patria* on September 7th, we must finish work on the chapel, ready for the bishop's visit. After that I hope not to make any more long journeys before term ends.

'I am only half way through this letter and it is nearly

midnight. I will break off now and finish it tomorrow. Poor *mãe ingleza:* struggling with her dictionary! . . .

'Back to my typewriter. I have just finished giving the children a singing lesson and they are playing outside. They really play now. The children in Cacimbas, especially, are a joy. There are fifty pupils now who have not missed a single day of school. The classes are held in the small patched-up chapel and when it comes to writing, the children have to kneel on the floor and write on the benches. During school hours we hang an old tarpaulin in front of the altar. If only we had a school building! The girls are longing to learn embroidery, but there is nowhere for them to work. Sewing-machines are out of the question at present, but if we could afford the stock of raw materials and a teacher, they could sit in the shade of a small cluster of *figueira* trees.

'A midwife, as you suggest, would be wonderful, but I fear life here is too hard. In spite of our road-building, most of her visits would have to be made on horseback. And who would pay her salary? And what of the brackish water she would have to use so much of the year? She would have to be nurse as well as midwife, of course.

'I would end this letter, but there is something else so urgent. You thought that Oxfam might be able to send us some clothes. I beg you to get in touch with them. We need clothing desperately, especially this year. The men working on the roads are almost naked. The shipment must be addressed to CRS, Salvador. If they are sent to Rio I shall never get them. Even from Salvador the transport of 1,000 kilos of old clothes would cost £80, but this would be really worth while. We are now in the period which is described here as 'cold'. It is the time when it is less hot. The daytime temperature varies from 25-30°, but at night it drops to 15° in some places. Most people sleep on the floor without covering, and there is a local saying, "fire is the blanket of the poor". They light a fire to escape the cold, the fire goes out and then many, especially older people, get influenza or pneumonia. With no doctor to help them it is easy to die. I can't afford to lose the clothes you mention, and the sooner they arrive, the better.'

The heavy shower of April 12th, whilst filling the excavation for the new reservoir, had not really moistened the sub-soil. By mid-July, only a third of the water remained, owing partly to evaporation and partly to seepage.

'Our water will run out in September when the heat is at its worst,' wrote the Padre. 'As soon as the reservoir is dry, we shall continue the excavation, hoping we have the whole of it dug out in time for the rains.'

10

ON August 5th, the Padre wrote from Rio de Janeiro, 'I arrived here a week ago and at once telephoned to your brother, Mr Benton. He received me immediately and I had the feeling that I was being welcomed not by an unknown diplomat but by an old friend, even a member of the family. He listened to everything I had to say with such interest. Two days later I lunched with him and his wife, Dona Peggie, and we talked from mid-day until three o'clock. I was captivated by her enthusiasm. I shall never forget our meeting. Apart from finding myself in surroundings quite different from those in which I live, an apartment of great luxury and yet so simple, I felt as though I were with my own countrymen. On the following day they came to the presbytery where I was staying and left me a present of great value. Unfortunately, I was out.

'Each day I went to CRS and watched the translation of my report. It is nearly finished and will be sent direct to Cafod by Mr Benton, instead of the normal slower routing via Geneva.

'It is wonderful how Father Leising's attitude has changed,

owing largely to his contact with you. He is still amazed that Oxfam should take such an interest in our work. The visit of Engineer Farias to the Fundação also helped.

'I left Rio for São Paulo and went to Santos once more. It was just as I thought. The whole delay over the crates has been caused by lack of a document certifying the existence of the Fundação. I took the document with me but I couldn't wait for the clothes to be cleared through the customs. It was five degrees below freezing point on the mountain road and I nearly died of cold in the bus, knowing that inside your crates was your warm sweater. How much I wanted it! However, the Mercedarian Fathers have now lent me a warm garment and no harm has been done.

'Dona Peggie is determined to visit the Fundação. I am really apprehensive about this as we have no water for washing nor any sanitary conveniences as yet.'

Muriel, meanwhile, was unremitting in her efforts on behalf of her 'Brazilian son'. She had gathered a group of friends, to help in raising money, and regular meetings were held in Winchester to report progress and discuss new ideas. These activities worried Padre Lira.

On September 26th he wrote, 'I think you work too hard for your age and I feel great remorse that the appearance of your Brazilian son should have made things more difficult. We were eight brothers and sisters, the eldest fifteen years old when my father died, two years after my mother. Now that at the age of forty-four I have found a second mother I don't want to be orphaned again, so I beg you not to do too much.

'We are very busy preparing the chapel at Curral Novo for the bishop's visit. The cost of work on the altar, besides that of altar cloths and so on, will be covered by the money sent by you and your friends.

'We are now drinking brackish water from the sub-soil, but the degree of salinity is not so high this year. With lemon juice it is tolerable, though one's liver objects to the constant acid.'

On September 26th the Padre wrote that the bishop's visit had been a great success. Two hundred children had made their first communion, and the number would have been doubled had there been roads for transporting the rest.

'Even before dawn the first truck arrived with a group of children. It was a wonderful sight, all of them in uniform with the badge of the Fundação and all of them wearing socks and shoes. This was a marvel for the forgotten wilderness of the sertão. We gave the children coffee as soon as they arrived, as most of them left home fasting and would not return until evening.

'At midnight there was mass for men only and more than fifty made their confession. Up till then, not a single man, with the exception of those about to be married, had ever come to confession. Three hundred men attended the service. There was no drinking, though they had spent the night out of doors, as we could not offer them any accommodation.

'On the next day there was mass for the women and girls, and the chapel simply could not hold them all. That afternoon, the bishop rested.

'Next day, the 24th, we held the Feast of Nossa Senhora das Mercês at the Fundação and mass was celebrated in the compound. The total number of communicants was over one thousand. I never expected such a blessing. The bishop and his priests were our guests at the Fundação and we gave lunch to over three hundred people, some of whom had ridden as much as a hundred kilometres. They were gruelling days and the heat was intense, but we were delighted to find that so many people had come uninvited, including various officials and the Prefect of São Raimundo. The only thing that worried the visitors was our brackish water.

'Your photograph was on view and I told people that it was thanks to this elderly lady and her group of friends that we had been able to repair the chapel and the altar, which looked beautiful and dignified. The children all wanted to see the "old lady" who had given the jeep to the Padre. Poor Oxfam! It was impossible to make the children understand what "Oxfam" meant.

'I am so glad your holiday was good. You describe the beauty of the small island in Brittany where your husband is buried as "bathed in sunshine". For us, a beautiful day is one in which the sky is heavy with clouds, clouds which will bring rain. At this time of the year the heat is insupportable. We are planting some trees and if they grow to give a little shade, the compound will be pleasanter.

'Hoping that I may get further help, I have taken the opportunity of buying fifty acres of land near Curral Novo including some beds of clay which should provide an impermeable lining for a future reservoir.

'I shall soon be taking the first consignment of embroidery to the South for sale. We are so short of water that, incredible as it may seem, the work has to be taken to Juazeiro to be washed.

'The crates have at last been released from Santos customs and are in São Paulo. A friend there will try to arrange free transport to Piauí.'

At the beginning of October the Padre wrote from São Paulo, 'Tomorrow I shall be flying back to my Piauí. Here it is pouring with rain but there so dry that one could weep.

'When I was in Rio I saw your brother once more and visited his home twice. I was received with great affection and Dona Peggie is becoming more and more interested in Piauí. We always talk of you. She plans to write a book about Brazil and now I am sure that they will visit the Fundação and see the results of all the help you have given me.'

A month later he described the end of the school year. 'It was really deeply touching to see the children in tears, not just because school would be shut for several months and there would be little to eat at home, but at the thought of leaving their teachers and missing their school-fellows. Last year when the professoras described this I thought they were exaggerating to comfort me in my illness. But it is true, and a wonderful encouragement.'

At the beginning of December, the Padre loaded the jeep with embroideries, bedspreads, napkins and tablecloths and set out on the long journey to São Paulo. The embroideries sold well, and the crates from Santos were awaiting him.

'I am so anxious to open the boxes, but the longer I wait the more I shall appreciate them. There is something so wonderful about a parcel. Money is an essential, but a package is something warm and personal, a real human exchange, a giving and a receiving.

'I shall divide my time from now to the beginning of February between Rio and São Paulo as there is so much to arrange in both cities. You ask why I buy my supplies in São Paulo instead of the nearer cities of Recife and Salvador. Even taking into account the expense of the journey this is an economy, as things are so much cheaper there. I go South in January and February when the schools are shut, and stock up. During the rest of the year, I ask people who are going down to bring me odd things.

'Brazilians are a restless people, always on the move, and it is easier to get around now. Fifteen years ago, the journey by the São Francisco River to Pirapora took about a fortnight. From there, one went on by train – to Rio in two days or São Paulo in three. Now, one can go by bus from Juazeiro to São Paulo and it only takes about five days. There is an aeroplane from Petrolina to Salvador twice a week too, but this is very expensive. So I go down by bus and sometimes I can get a free air ticket back. [This was in the days when Brazilian air lines were, in fact, very cheap and tickets were handed out freely to politicians and state employees, who often passed them on to their friends.]

'Your brother has just told me that Oxfam and Cafod between them are making a grant of £2,208 for machinery for the shoe factory and that Cafod will give a further £400 towards the cost of building reservoirs. What wonderful support from England! I heard, too, that the clothes from Oxfam have arrived in Recife. Salvador would have been nearer, but I can fetch the clothes when I go to Recife in March or April.

'I left two embroidered tablecloths with Mr Benton for you, also the goatskin.'

The Padre spent Christmas with the Spanish nuns in the old people's home at Lençois Paulista 300 kilometres from São Paulo. 'I came in the jeep, driving it myself! This house is in the middle of the sugar-cane fields and very silent. The Sisters are wonderful, though they try to make me eat too much.

'I have kind and generous patrons in the town, especially the leading family who built this old people's home. They have two large mills producing two million sacks of sugar a year. When I leave, the jeep will be loaded with soap, biscuits, wine and all sorts of wonderful gifts for the Fundação, and when the lorry comes down to fetch the machinery for the shoe factory it will pass through Lençois and pick up fifty sacks of sugar.

'I shall take this opportunity of having a check-up too, as the "machine" must be in good order for the year's work. What a different Christmas this is from last. Then I was ill and discouraged. Now, everything is happiness.'

11

THE year 1967 started badly for the North-East. In Piauí, the scanty rains of December did not moisten the soil sufficiently to allow the crops to be sown, and by the end of January no more rain had fallen.

The Padre wrote from São Paulo, 'The experts fear that a new cycle of drought like that of the 'fifties is beginning. In 1961, a series of good winters began and lasted up to 1964, when it rained as never before. 1966 was a dry year and 1967 promises to be even worse. Pray God that the Bentons do not visit us in a period of drought or they will have a bitter impression of our region. I long for the silence and peace of Piauí.'

A month later the Padre wrote from Rio, 'I have just returned from São Paulo. The results of my check-up were better than I expected. The stomach ulcer has healed, probably because I stuck to the letter of my diet. The hernia in my throat has improved, though there are signs of varicose veins there and the doctor has given me a prescription in case haemorrhage should occur. The blood test, unfortunately, revealed some amoebas and this means drinking as much milk as possible, and taking a lot of medicines. These are expensive, though my consultations were free.

'The money for the shoe factory has not yet arrived, which is surprising as it was sent at the end of January, but here again we have benefited, since the value of the pound in Brazil has meantime risen by twenty per cent.

'I have wonderful news about the machinery. The owner of a factory in Franca, so-called capital of the shoe industry, has died and his widow is selling the equipment for Cr$30,000, to be paid in instalments. I offered Cr$12,000 cash down, and to my surprise the offer was accepted. A real gift from Providence! There are nineteen machines, some of them almost new and all in good condition, and I have until the end of the month to find the money. I hope it will have arrived by then.

'Whilst in São Paulo I met Dom Helder Camara who, contrary to my expectations, promised me substantial help. He acts as liaison for the Alliance for Progress which conducts all its business in Recife. I must go there as soon as possible and can, at the same time, pick up the clothes from Oxfam. [Unfortunately, nothing came of this promising contact with Dom Helder.]

'I heard from São Raimundo that a little rain had fallen, but I don't know what has happened in Curral Novo, the driest spot in the whole region. There have been food riots in the cities of the North-East and the Government has sent relief. This will never happen in the caatinga because our people just die quietly and never resort to violence, so our droughts make no impression on the authorities.'

The money from England finally arrived and at the end of February the Padre went to Franca with Engineer Farias to examine the machinery. Owing to a general shortage of ready money the Padre was able to buy the whole contents of the factory, including tables, chairs, trolleys and a thousand lasts, for Cr$10,000, just over a third of its agreed value. Senhor Silvio, doyen of the shoe manufacturers in the town, agreed to pack and house the machinery until it could be fetched.

'The truck will have to make three journeys and the last load will only reach the Fundação in May,' wrote the Padre. 'As soon as I return I must see to building the workshop – and to finding the money to do so. A technician from Franca will spend a year at the Fundação to teach the apprentices. He is a man of over fifty with a very good reputation. If all goes well, the factory will contribute substantially to the economic development of the region.'

In March, Muriel wrote to the Padre that she was coming to

Rio to stay with her brother, but that in view of her health it had been decided that she should not undertake the arduous journey to the Fundação. The Padre's reply was ecstatic.

'Shall I be able to come to Rio to meet you? Only death would prevent me. Your visit is the one thing needed to crown the many blessings that I have received since you crossed my path.

'And now I have good news for you. The rains have come, fine and constant instead of the usual brief, torrential downpours, and there will be a better harvest than for many years. The reservoir is full and we should have drinking water until August, at least.

'Another joy. The clothes have arrived and, to my surprise, 100 kilos of medicines, from the States. I hope that they include vitamins, which are essential in view of the present malnutrition. Please thank Oxfam for their wonderful help in arranging this shipment.'

The term started at the beginning of May. Enrolment for 1967 at the Fundação showed a 20% increase of pupils. Cacimbas now had ninety children, all between seven and fourteen years old. Another school was being opened at Barra do Bonito.

'The teachers for both of the outlying schools were trained here, only a primary course, but the first fruits of our work. For me, this is an intense joy.

'We are no longer isolated from the outside world. Every week trucks from Juazeiro come over the new roads to trade. On the way to Barra they pass the Fundação and one can buy sugar, coffee and all sorts of things. This is real progress. In June we shall use the Food for Peace supplied by Caritas to continue our road-building programme – 150 kilometres more this year, we hope. One road will lead to the chapel of Ponta da Serra, built by the Jesuits in the seventeenth century, and we hope to repair this and use it on weekdays as a school.

'After all our anxiety, the winter was wonderful. It rained

until May – something which has never happened before. People say that since a priest came to the area the droughts have broken. I would hate to disillusion them, but I fear that their optimism is ill-founded. Work on our reservoir has been held up by the rain and is only now under way. It is a rather specialised job and a gang has to be brought from São Raimundo to do it.

'The machinery for the shoe factory is all here and in perfect condition. One of the machines weighs more than a ton. What a miracle, *meu Deus*! People come from far and wide to see. We still have to build the workshop but money is the problem. I hope, though, that we shall have the factory working by the end of the year.

'Last Sunday, the second in May, we celebrated Mothers' Day and the First Communion. The toys which you and your kind friends sent were eagerly sought after, especially the dolls.'

On June 13th the Padre wrote that Engineer Farias had spent five days at the Fundação in order to make the report on the water problem requested by Cafod.

'He suggested building a reservoir at Cacimbas which, with its school of ninety pupils, is one of the communities most in need of water; another at Curral Novo, the largest hamlet, and the completion of the reservoir at the Fundação.

'I spent some anxious days because of the threat of war in the Middle East and suspended work on the factory building in case England should be involved and we should be cut off from further funds. But now the situation appears to have returned to normal and the work continues. We have started a novena for peace to Nossa Senhora das Mercês.

'Work on our reservoir is proceeding apace. Owing to seepage from the previous excavation Engineer Farias has stipulated that the basin must be lined with concrete. Using the grant from Cafod, the depth of the reservoir can be doubled, which will reduce the proportionate loss from evaporation, but Farias says that if we are to have a sufficient supply of water the area must also be increased.

'The Bank of Brazil in Remanso has agreed to finance the factory building until the money arrives which we hope to get from the Alliance for Progress [a hope which was not fulfilled] and we have just had a visit from the manager and two chief accountants. They came in our jeep and appeared impressed with all that they saw. We are so anxious to get the factory working, not only for the sake of the boys, but also to provide an independent income for the Fundação.

'I fear that I must ask you not to send any more medicines. The customs officials insist that each one must be unwrapped and examined separately by a doctor. I managed to persuade them this time that it was a waste of effort, but next time they will not let me off. Furthermore they will charge me for the doctor's time.

'I have had a letter confirming the arrival of the Bentons on July 9th. Besides the profound happiness it will give us all, I feel that their visit will help to make our modest work more widely understood.

'I am arranging a *Concentração*, or gathering of people from all over the "parish". Word has been going round for some time now and we expect two or three hundred. They will ride in, some for two days or more, and sleep in the open air and we shall give them all a meal.

'And then, on August 17th or 18th, I shall be in Rio for the supreme joy of embracing my English mother. I intend to stay a week there.'

PART TWO

Close-Up

12

UNTIL our unexpected transfer to Brazil in May 1966 Padre Lira was to us a shadowy figure – someone of concern to my sister-in-law Muriel; one of the many requiring an introduction or a routine donation from time to time.

When we arrived in Rio he seemed almost as remote from the careless teeming life of the city as from the cathedral town of Winchester, but the situation had altered. We were now able to be of direct help – or at least try to be. Our position had changed from spectators to possible collaborators.

The Brazilian public was aware of the general problems of the North-East: the poverty, the ignorance and the latifundian economy. The recurrent droughts of the region led to mass migration and food riots followed by relief measures, and the occasional floods in the sugar belt on the coast resulted in sporadic appeals for charity.

The Government were concerned about the problems of the North-East, but their interest seemed to stop short of the silent, meagre south-eastern regions of Piauí. A great stretch of country like this, without access to the mass media of communication and possessing nothing which others would want to exploit, is of as much interest to the public and the administration as the surface of the moon before the age of the astronauts.

All the other States of the North-East possess cities of some importance and areas which, properly administered, could become prosperous, but Piauí is like a bleached mutton bone without a scrap of meat.

None of our friends could give us any information about it. Once we heard a comedian in a night club announce a first prize of a fortnight's free holiday in Piauí – second prize, three weeks. For a State larger than Great Britain this seemed rather scant public mention.

Brazil, from the days of the first Portuguese settlers, has been handicapped by its very size and potential wealth. The soil along the coasts of the North-East runs for hundreds of kilometres rich and black, and the rainfall there is adequate for growing the sugar which was so highly valued in the past. Settlers were relatively few. The native Indians would not adapt themselves to any form of organised labour and quietly withdrew into the forests, but the supply of slaves from the coasts of Africa was unlimited. So, apparently, was the supply of land.

Forests were felled, burned, planted, harvested and abandoned as soon as the fertile top soil was washed away or exhausted. Sooner or later world markets for a given product were captured by countries with more sophisticated methods of cultivation, but there was always another boom crop and another landowner to send his gangs in to rape the forest, so there was little incentive to settle and enrich the land. Human values were of little account and the men of the caatinga were perhaps fortunate in their freedom to die of natural causes.

Nowadays, a more enlightened government is facing an almost overwhelming task in trying to heal the wounds of the past. An official agency, the Superintendency for the Development of the North-East, commonly known as Sudene, was set up in 1959 to tempt industry into the area by an ingenious system of tax concessions to investors, but centuries of mismanagement cannot be put right in a single generation.

It was a cool winter day in August when Padre Lira walked into our flat in Rio, the leathery pock-marked skin of his face contrasting with his pale tropical cassock, frayed with constant pounding in the brackish water of the caatinga.

He sat down in one of the massive armchairs provided by the Ministry of Works and opened his heavy leather briefcase.

'For you, Dona Peggie,' he said and handed me a beautiful piece of embroidery with the warm smile of a man for whom giving means so much more than receiving. His left eye drooped a little from a slight cast, and long exposure to the scorching sun had etched deep lines round his mouth and eyes. His cropped dark hair was thick and slightly grizzled, and his whole aspect suggested purpose and endurance.

We talked for many hours of his plans and problems and how we could best help him to contact organisations which might be of use. Even a short acquaintance with the authorities had shown us that an application, to be successful, must have influential support.

The Padre showed us photographs of the Fundação and of his people taken by Padre Lorenz, a German former Benedictine monk, who had been his tutor in the seminary at Salvador, and who was now working as chaplain in the docks at Niteroi across the harbour.

'When you visit the Fundação I will invite Padre Lorenz too. His photographs are wonderful and he is going to experiment with a cine camera. He has a hard life in Rio, but in the caatinga he finds peace and everyone loves his company.'

13

At a quarter to five the alarm clock rang in the darkness. It was Monday, July 10th. Outside on the landing the luggage was stacked ready to go to the airport. We had worked all through the day before sorting and packing the things for our visit to the Fundação and weighing the result, since excess baggage to Petrolina, where we were to spend the night, cost six shillings a kilo. About twenty pounds' weight was stuffed into the camera case and a couple of string bags, which we would carry in our hands. It is a strange fact of air travel in

Latin America that the smaller the aeroplane, the bigger the amount of luggage you are allowed to take into the cabin.

A couple of large sacks filled with old clothes and a crate of food and sweets were clearly labelled 'Padre Lira, Fundação Ruralista' in the hope of softening the hearts of the officials at the check-in. For ourselves, we were taking minimum clothing. The rest of the space in our suitcases was filled with presents for Padre Lira, Alcibiades and the professoras, as well as dress patterns, embroidery magazines, medicines and so on.

It was still dark when we reached the airport on the harbour edge in the centre of Rio, but as we crossed the tarmac to the twin-engined plane the sunrise tore fiery streaks out of the leaden sky. While the plane circled the bay and the Sugar Loaf, still strung with the lights of the cable railway, the sun broke clear of the sea.

I love flying in small aeroplanes with their slow pace and the fascinating details of the land one sees below. In spite of an exploding population, large parts of Brazil are still empty, and we looked down on mile after mile of coast with malachite lagoons roped together by a golden sand bar while the land stretched deserted to the mountains beyond.

The airport of Vitoria is small and busy, and even equipped with souvenirs for sale. Friendly ground staff took us into their office to study a detailed map of the coast. They showed us the course of the iron ore trains from Rio Doce in the interior, where deposits of the high-grade mineral are greater than those of the Ruhr, to the newly-built port of Tuberão. After the chill of our twin-engined plane it was pleasant to drink a *cafezinho* (the ubiquitous small cup of black Brazilian coffee) in the sun beside the gay flower beds.

The country after Vitoria was beautiful, with cushions of forest between lush pastures bounded by the chain of coastal lagoons. Here and there, a breach in the sand bar would release a great earthy stain as a river flowed into the blue of the sea.

Around Itabuna the forest retreated before the neat ranks of the cocoa plantations. This land was cleared at a cost of considerable bloodshed during the savage rivalries of the gangs employed by the big landowners which only came to an end about forty years ago.

A lambswool scatter of cloud veiled the land, and then the mist closed down. Through rifts we glimpsed the Bay of Todos os Santos and then we swung in to land at Salvador de Bahia, where we were allowed three quarters of an hour for lunch.

Taking a yet smaller aeroplane we turned inland towards empty country, more and more desolate as we crossed the sertão of Bahia. Right to the horizon stretched the scrub, with occasional small hills to lessen the monotony. Like a raw red weal, the newly-made highway from Feira de Santana to Petrolina ran below us in a straight line.

Road-building in Brazil is like a gigantic operation of plastic surgery. Mountain sides are carved away, ravines filled, landscapes transformed in an astonishingly short space of time. Dual carriageways are replaced by separate up-and-down roads on each side of steep mountain valleys. Whole stretches of sea are filled in and turned into boulevards and new beaches. From Brasilia great roads stretch starfish-wise to the Amazon, the north-east coast, to all the great cities, to the Mato Grosso and to the Andes.

Once the forest is felled and the road bed laid, the first buses start off on journeys of two, three and four days, smothered in red dust, manhandled out of the mud during the rains. Passengers sling their hammocks beneath wayside trees or lie on the ground beside the new-style covered wagons. They bring their own food and drink – and their guns. Not long after this, the road is already metalled, Pullman buses with a hostess, a shower and a loo are making scheduled runs and the dwindling Indian tribes have withdrawn still further into the forests.

At the clean small airport of Petrolina a deputation was waiting to welcome us. After greetings all round, we discovered that it consisted of Alcibiades, the Padre's uncle, a small man with innocent eyes, silver hair and a skin burnished like a hazel-nut by wind and sun; Monsenhor Nestor, headmaster of a secondary school in Remanso and a former pupil with Padre Lira at the seminary at Salvador, and fat dusky Senhor Pedro, a shopkeeper from São Raimundo described as 'a good friend of the Fundação'.

Muriel's jeep stood proudly outside the airport andb eside it, an old Willys Rural lent by Senhor Pedro to help in transporting our group and the luggage.

Glare from the dusty ground stung one's eyes and the heat struck like a blow. A bumpy few hundred yards took us past the station of the narrow-gauge railway which runs erratically for 550 kilometres in a northerly direction to Teresina, capital of the State of Piauí. Unfortunately, it passes nowhere near the Fundação.

On our left lay the cemetery, high-walled like a miniature Kremlin with colour-washed tombs huddled secretively within. In many sad little towns in the North-East the cemetery, with its small tended plots and sheltering walls is an oasis amid the squalor of the empty streets, but Petrolina is a cheerful place.

It was the weekly market day and our hosts promised that we should explore, but first we would go to the Neumann Hotel, which has outsmarted its rival in the older town of Juazeiro on the opposite bank of the São Francisco River.

Although we had been warned not to expect too much, our hearts sank as we walked into the hotel entrance, a fly-blown café open to the street. Behind the café was a patio with bedrooms opening directly into it and a rough shower for people who rode in travel-stained from the dusty roads. Above, an open gallery gave access to a further row of bedrooms. At one end, over the café, was a dining room.

Our bedroom was small and devoid of furniture but for two very hard beds, each with a single sheet and a cotton coverlet.

When our luggage was piled up against the blotchy walls there was just room to move. A small cubicle next door held a cold-water shower, erratic and rusty, but nevertheless a great luxury.

After a quick wash we joined the group in the street below. We had seen many poor and exiguous markets but never one quite so sparse. After the gleaming flesh of even the poor in Bahia these people seemed dusty and tinder dry. There was no sense of squalor, no hidden sores as on the coast, but even the fruit and vegetables laid in small heaps on the ground for sale, were stunted. In a side street people clustered round some pushcarts with ragged awnings, buying platefuls of dingy stew, and even the merchandise in the more prosperous stalls was of the cheapest.

Since foreigners are rare in Petrolina, our interest was returned, but there was no resentment of our cameras as amongst the Andean people.

I halted with the Monsenhor to chat with an old man selling dried herbs and berries from the mato. Asked to describe his wares, he explained that this herb was for *grippe*, that a vermifuge, some sedative, others for poulticing broken limbs.

'Are there any for *candomblé*?' I asked.

'No,' he replied warily, 'these are medicinal only.'

Later I was told that *candomblé*, the north-eastern version of the religion brought to Brazil by the African slaves, was practised in the twin towns.

From the market, we drove through the town, admiring the small public gardens bedded out with soil brought from the fertile lands, and the cathedral built by a French bishop – a rustic Lisieux where birds circled the white-washed vaults in aerial trespass.

'Ten years ago there was nothing at Petrolina,' said Alcibiades. 'Now we have an airport and a refinery for vegetable oil and the place is growing all the time.'

A short road from the cathedral led down to the edge of the São Francisco, sleepily shining between its wide banks. An iron bridge, which pauses on an island in mid-stream, carries road and railway to Juazeiro on the opposite bank.

Juazeiro is the terminus of the riverine navigation from Pirapora some 1,500 kilometres upstream. Although steamers ply no further downstream, the São Francisco still has some 1,200 kilometres to flow before it reaches the sea, but navigation is impeded by rapids and the spectacular hydro-electric works at the Paulo Afonso dam.

The jeep bucketed up the ramp to a track which ran beside the rails as they crossed the bridge. Great rivers far from the sea have an air of mystery, of a purpose known only to themselves. Cutting across state boundaries they preserve their own characters, and a life grows up around them which is something apart.

'Before the bridge was built,' said Alcibiades, 'one crossed the river by boat. It was beautiful. The men sang as they rowed. There was no hurry then.'

We were bumping down the ramp at the far end and into the dusty streets of Juazeiro. Across the water, the white spire of the cathedral rose above the houses of Petrolina. Below us, a lorry up to its axles in water was being bathed by its sunburnt owner.

Lacking the thrust of Petrolina, Juazeiro has an old-fashioned provincial air, even to the cathedral and the prim little 'palace' of the bishop. Strange that two cathedrals and two bishops should stare at one another across the water, but the situation arose because each town belonged to a different state.

We were told later that the inhabitants would like to combine the two into a single town called Jualina, which would be the capital of a new State of São Francisco embracing the poorest and most neglected parts of Bahia, Pernambuco and Piauí. It is curious that three poor men should imagine that by being together they would become richer, but they maintain that, if the funds due to these regions for education, health services and road-building actually reached them and they were allowed to administer their own local taxation, they would be considerably better off.

Our ears were ringing from the noise of the flight and our eyes and throats were dry from glare and dust.

'Let's stop for a beer at the Saldanho Marinho,' suggested Senhor Pedro.

So the jeep drew up at an old paddle-steamer, the first to ply the river, which had been lifted onto the quay and is used as part monument, part simple restaurant. The upper deck is covered by a shabby awning and three or four tables have been squeezed into the tiny cabin below. A wood-burning galley is perched in the waist of the boat where fuel for the boiler was formerly stored.

As we drank our beer the sun sank over the infinite beckoning of the river and the gaily-painted paddle-steamers moored along the bank, while *Miss São Francisco*, loaded to the gunwale with sacks, barrels and goats, crept upstream against the current.

'How long does it take from here to Pirapora?' I asked.

'About a week down and ten days up. Though there is no timetable. Last week one of the steamers was lost. Nothing was heard for days. Perhaps the captain had a little friend . . .' Senhor Pedro winked at the Monsenhor.

'Not all the craft are as old as these,' he continued, looking at the showboat-type paddle-steamers below. 'We have boats with diesel motors as well as stern-wheelers. Why, we even have a tourist vessel, clean, with showers and a swimming pool on board . . .' He seemed pleased with his story.

'Where is she now?' I enquired.

'Well – we don't have any timetable, you see.'

Back at the hotel, several parties of men, sunburnt and brisk-looking, were already eating dinner. As always in Brazil, food was brought to the table on numbers of separate dishes, though portions in this part of the world were tiny compared with those in the South.

To avoid the worst of the heat we planned to leave at 4 a.m. next day on the 200-kilometre trip to the Fundação, but this was gradually whittled down to six sharp.

A fine chill air struck through the cotton coverlet and snores and dry coughing echoed round the patio. I was awakened from light sleep by the crowing of a cock. Darkness, and our clock had stopped. A long time passed and my bones ached on the hard bed. Drowsing once more, I was torn out of sleep by the cock, a compulsive self-advertiser, or one of a gang working in shifts.

A flea, or so I hoped, was busy on my ribs. Later, a man arrived and stamped into the room next door. A drowsy spell, and the dogs started barking. When someone knocked on our door I was already nearly dressed, since I knew that country people seldom allow one more time for getting ready than it takes to pull on a pair of trousers.

Coffee was already being served, at 5.30 a.m., to all the guests of the night before. We refused meal porridge and ate an egg swimming in oil, *linguiça*, a hard gristly sausage, and some tallowy cheese with slabs of unleavened bread.

Dawn was breaking and Alcibiades had not yet appeared from his house near the railway station. Finally it was decided to go and fetch him, but when we reached his front door, which was barred by a low table carrying an ash tray, we found that he had gone to the hotel by another route.

At last, only half an hour late, we set out on the wide federal highway in the direction of Remanso. Alcibiades and Monsenhor Nestor, arms linked against the jolting, sat in front and we on the rear seat where, it was alleged, we should ride a little smoother.

The road was wide with a firm core and a covering of loose stones. One day, when funds were released, it would receive a coating of asphalt, but unfortunately the first thirty kilometres ran through the State of Pernambuco, which was allegedly hard up and Bahia, which carries the rest, had already shot its bolt over the hard-top from Feira de Santana to Petrolina.

Passing the vegetable oil refinery and a new trade school, we were at once in the caatinga, empty scrub country with odd twisted trees, and every so many kilometres a single house built of mud bricks or wattle and daub. Under the huge sky the road ran into the empty distance. Occasionally a lonely pig, somehow involved in pressing business on the other side of the road, would scamper across under our wheels. Sometimes a pale zebu cow with serrated hump, long ears and frill upon frill of dewlap, stared from the mato, warily guarding a small calf.

From time to time we saw goats, intent on self-preservation, with forefeet seeking a grip on a slender trunk so that their leathery lips could snatch at the branches of a tree which could not grow fast enough to elude them. Here in the caatinga though, the goats had at last met their match.

For most of the year the vegetation is so dessicated and thorny that it is not stripped bare. Under the burning sun the leaves soon fall, to be devoured by the goats like the paper bags of visitors to the London Zoo. When, after the rains, the bone-pale branches crack into clusters of leaf and blossom, the goats have not time for the war of attrition which has devastated countries where the vegetation remains green.

But they have other resources. The fat, pentagonal sections of the mandacarú cactus, used as cattle fodder after singeing to remove the spines, are devoured entirely by these animals. Their mouths and tongues must have a certain softness like our own, and yet they seem immune to the tearing of the thorns. Where the catingueiro uses leather to protect his flesh, the goat will take into his mouth thorns so burningly pointed that a chance touch will make one shrink with pain.

'The goats love the poisonous favela,' said Alcibiades. 'While the other animals are dying, they become fat on it.'

'The goats of the caatinga give the best meat in the whole of Brazil,' observed Monsenhor Nestor. 'Since they live on aromatic plants, the flesh has none of the usual disagreeable flavour. You will see.'

We came to a pond beside the road, the turgid greenish water framed in trampled mud and the whole enclosed in a palisade.

'People come here from miles away to fetch the water. Would you like to stop and look?'

A boy, the rough gates shut carefully behind him, was filling his clay pot. Two girls came walking out of the distance with large rusty tins on their heads.

'But do they drink this water?' I enquired. 'It looks filthy, even if the fence does keep out the animals.'

'This is drinking water for the whole neighbourhood,' said Alcibiades, 'perhaps half a dozen families in a radius of four or five kilometres. As long as the water doesn't dry up they are only too happy. When I have to drink from a pool like this I spread out my handkerchief and drink through it. Like that you swallow no mud or living creatures.' Except bacteria, I thought, though perhaps these may be held in check by an immunity acquired over the years.

It was not yet seven, but the light was so harsh that all but the driver had retired behind their sun glasses. The girls by now had filled their tins, giggling at the foreigners who seemed to find this operation interesting, and were walking away upright and graceful beneath their heavy loads.

A rider with a leather hat, a cotton sack and a gun slung over his shoulder, came towards us on a small, dusty horse.

'He's a *caboclo*,' said Monsenhor Nestor.

Now the word *caboclo*, like so many other words in Brazil, is used rather vaguely. Michaelis' dictionary gives the meaning as 'a civilised Brazilian of pure Indian blood; a Brazilian half-breed part white, part Indian; any copper-coloured mulatto with straight hair; a frontiersman, inlander, ranger; an agricultural labourer, farm hand; a treacherous fellow'. Alcibiades and Monsenhor Nestor opted a little uncertainly for a half-breed of white and Indian blood.

By the side of the highway, a rough tent, made of a tarpaulin stretched over a single rope between two trees, sheltered a road gang. Outside, a fire was burning and two bicycles were stacked against a tree, a startling sight in this country of horses. This explained the little rings of ash and charred tree stumps which we were to see at intervals along the road. Apart from felling wood to light fires, the activities of the gang apparently only consisted in shovelling some loose stones into the larger holes in the road's surface.

'The Prefect of Casa Nova is a good man. He does his best for the roads,' observed Alcibiades solemnly.

We passed through a cluster of small houses, one even brick-faced and painted pink and blue.

'The Canadian Fathers run a mission here. They are friends with the Prefect,' said Monsenhor Nestor. 'The Bishop of Juazeiro, Thomas Murphy is an American. He is a good man and a liberal, not like the Bishop of São Raimundo who is in charge of your area. Still, I suppose they are thankful to have anyone. The last bishop stayed three days and then hurried back to Spain.'

I remarked on the silvery look of the mato so soon after the last, and exceptional, rains had fallen in May.

'It is not really dry here,' I was told. 'Wait until you get into the region of Curral Novo. That is the driest part of the caatinga and the Fundação is in its centre.'

Suddenly the emptiness ahead was interrupted. Men were engaged in building a bridge to carry the road over a water-course. On the left of the road was a plantation of vines, dazzlingly green.

'This riacho, like every other, turns into a torrent during the rainy season. The owner of this land is a rich man – he has the monopoly for sacramental port all over the region. So he built a dam at his own expense, but after the rains the road was submerged,' explained Alcibiades. We were bumping along the edge of a small sheet of water and across the top of the dam.

'Now the State of Bahia is building a bridge for the road and everyone will be better off. Any improvements have to be started privately and you are lucky if the State doesn't put obstacles in your way. Bahia is better than Piauí, of course,' Alcibiades added.

A few patches of vegetables were growing near the water, jealously fenced against the animals. As well as the shortage of water, the need to enclose restricts the areas which can be planted. Staves for the fences must be hacked from the mato and trimmed, and then driven into the hard ground almost touching one another.

'In other countries where the stock runs wild a wire fence can be put up in a few hours,' said Alcibiades, 'but money is hardly used in these parts. The wood is there for the taking. The labour of a man's wife and children costs him nothing, but where would he get the cash for wire?'

'So the livestock wanders about without any restriction?' I asked Alcibiades.

'Quite freely. You could never fence them all in. The cattle are branded with a hot iron and the sheep and goats have their ears notched to show their owner.'

'And do people never change the markings or steal the animals?'

'The catingueiros are renowned for their honesty and will look after a stray animal perhaps for years until its owner comes to claim it,' said Monsenhor Nestor. 'Any young born to it will be marked with the same unknown brand. If an animal has to be slaughtered its exact value will be returned to the owner if he appears. To call a man a cattle thief is a terrible insult; worse if you talk of goats, and "chicken thief" is the worst insult of all.'

We had reached a petrol pump flanked by a small café and a hut or two clustered round a T-junction. Here we would turn north-west towards Piauí.

While the tank was being filled we went into the café, dark after the blinding light outside. Cafezinhos were served, from a thermos flask this time. A small tank fixed to the wall behind the counter supplied water to the kitchen behind. A tube, suspended by wires from the rafters, led to a small hand basin. Rinsing one's fingers was a luxury in this dry country.

'Where do you get the water?' the Monsenhor asked the proprietor.

'From a well 150 metres deep. You see the pump house across the road.'

'And the water's not salt?'

'No, thank God.' The man was obviously proud of his tiny café, named the Alvorada after the President's palace in Brasilia. On the counter a pan of water was bubbling over a Primus stove, because even in a small café in Brazil the cups are washed in boiling water. Gritty looking pieces of corn cake were protected by a wire cover, but some small slabs of goat's cheese lay beside them so black with flies as to resemble a French *tome au raisin* cheese with its coating of grape pips.

'I shall buy one of these for you to taste,' announced Alcibiades kindly.

The owner took us outside to see his vegetable garden which, like all those we afterwards saw in the caatinga, consisted of a rough table made with tree trunks and unstripped branches. The top, which measured three or four square yards, was covered with a layer of earth and on this were growing a few onions, beetroots and cabbage plants.

'These onions are acid,' explained the owner. 'The white sweet onions must be planted in the ground but we can't grow those here. The soil is too hot.'

Besides lifting the precious vegetables out of reach of the animals, the table garden gives their roots a rather cooler surrounding than the baking earth below.

We were shown some tomato plants supported by the fence around a plot of manioc, and a calabash with a few large gourds hanging from its withered branches.

'Those are used for carrying water, or cut in half to make bowls. You can't eat the pulp. It's sour and has to be scraped and rinsed out.'

We turned into a narrow dirt road. 'This is a municipal

road,' explained Alcibiades, 'built by the Prefect of Casa Nova. It runs for nine and a half leagues to the border of Piauí and there it stops.'

'There everything stops,' muttered Monsenhor Nestor.

'And that is where Padre Lira took over, I suppose. How much is a league?' I asked.

'Six kilometres,' replied Alcibiades. 'There was nothing but a mule track after the State border, and only a cart track from Curral Novo to São Raimundo Nonato – and São Raimundo itself is the back of beyond.'

We were now bucking along, with the mato close on either hand.

'They took a grader over this road,' said Alcibiades. 'It is not too bad, though the jeep jumps around a bit.' A fox flickered out of the bushes and across the road.

'There's a lot of rabies amongst the foxes,' Alcibiades commented. 'The other day a man near the Fundação was bitten. It is difficult to deal with a case like that.'

'Do you have serum?'

'No, and it's a long way to the nearest doctor – 120 kilometres over the bad road to São Raimundo. And before you hear that someone's been bitten it's probably too late . . .'

The road was running over sand, sometimes deep yellow and sometimes white. From time to time we crossed an outcrop of rock, the jolts making the bolting sing.

Great termites' nests clung, red-brown and crusted, to the tree trunks or stood like horrid monuments on the earth. Many of these nests remain abandoned for years and travellers sometimes break them open and use the domed upper part, reversed, as a cooking pot. I have always wanted to open an empty termite's nest, but our group showed no enthusiasm for this project.

The road wound on through the empty mato, up and down, curve after curve, since it followed the line of least resistance and there was no question of levelling anything but the actual surface. At one point we passed a lonely wooden cross, fenced like any other treasure, though with tiny stakes. An accident? Or the grave of someone too weak to reach the 'parrot's cage' lorry taking refugees from a drought to the distant city?

We had been jolting in the heat for four hours now and our skin and hair were dingy with dust. As we drove, I questioned Monsenhor Nestor and he gave me with endless patience the name of each tree and bush. Sometimes Alcibiades added a scrap of medicinal lore or some traditional knowledge of bird or beast. Unlike the *Carioca*, the inhabitant of Rio, to whom plants and flowers are all anonymous, the native-born catingueiro knows and uses every leaf and berry. Sometimes we stopped to pick a dried flower or some of the beautiful, dessicated golden seed pods.

In contrast to Padre Lira, who, at our first meeting had protested laughing, 'You are asking more questions than I do in the confessional, Dona Peggie,' the Monsenhor, a born teacher, appeared to enjoy one's interest.

A flock of sheep, long-legged and angular, their coats a little ill-fitting, ambled across the road to cluster beneath a silvery tree covered with flame-coloured blossom.

'Is that a form of flamboyant?' I asked.

'The tree is an umburana and the leaves have fallen already, but the flowers belong to the climbing *parasita* and unless this is removed it will gradually smother the tree,' Amongst the flowers I could see pale green leaves like mistletoe.

The road dipped and we passed a pond, the sky lying in it a dazzling blue against the parched caatinga.

'We will stop at Aramarí and visit Colonel Mariano. He is ninety-one years old and he will never forgive us if we don't.'

In the North-East 'Colonel' is an honorary title which has nothing to do with military rank, and was even occasionally bought by the big landowners. Here it was merely a matter of courtesy.

On a small rise stood a low white-washed house with

Aramarí painted above the door. Frangipani, oleander, hibiscus and datura peeped over the top of a walled enclosure.

'The senhora made that garden,' said Alcibiades, seeing my interest. 'She gives cuttings to the Fundação.' I thought of all the water which must be patiently carried up from the pool below.

On a narrow terrace outside the house stood a tall old man wearing a black cloak, clean blue shirt, grey cloth cap and pink bedroom slippers. His deep-set eyes were black and a great nose hooked over to brush his lips. One gnarled hand held a large stick.

Ninety-one is a respectable age in any country, but here where the average life-span of a man is only thirty-five years it is impressive. The jeep drew up in the scant shadow of a feathery tree and we were led forward and presented as 'the English'.

'Dona Peggie is writing a book,' added Monsenhor Nestor.

'Then you must send me a copy,' said Colonel Mariano.

'But does the Senhor Coronel read English?' I asked.

'English is no use to me,' he replied loftily, though one doubted whether in Portuguese he could read more than his name.

'But will you put Aramarí in your book?' I assured him that I would.

'And will you take my photograph?' enquired the Colonel.

'You are against the light. If the Senhor Coronel would like to step down from the terrace and stand before that tree . . .'

'My legs have failed me,' he replied with great dignity, though he was standing erect on softly swollen feet.

In reply to an enquiry by Monsenhor Nestor he told us that the pond was the result of a dam made in 1960, though this was the first year that it had held water. Beside it, in a small enclosure, stood a plantation of maize and manioc together with the jagged leaves and soft prickly berries of castor oil plants whose seeds would be sent to the refinery in Petrolina.

'You must come and sit down,' said Colonel Mariano. The

front of the house was almost cool in the shadow while the sunlight struck golden sparks from a false pepper tree and bounced brightly from the surface of the water.

We explained that we were late, that Padre Lira was anxiously expecting us at the Fundação, and that we had another two or three hours to go. The old man shook his head.

A goatskin stretched over crossed staves like a kite hung from a tree. To its neighbour a donkey was tethered and a pig, wearing a heavy wooden trapezium evidently designed to keep its head out of somewhere, bustled down the slope.

'Sit down, sit down,' repeated the old man, but it was arranged that we would call again on our return, and so we shook hands with each member of the family in turn, led by a silver-haired placid woman who I felt to be the creator of all that was beautiful at Aramarí. Beside her the sons and daughters, grandchildren and their babies appeared brutish as they thronged from the dark interior. This was the first of many mass hand-shakings, and one shrank instinctively from skin which could be washed so seldom, and from the flies which clustered round the eyes of the pale babies.

'I can't control my dislike of shaking hands,' confided the Monsenhor afterwards. 'Sick people insist on it. They are offended if you don't. I ought not to mind but . . .'

The tiny oasis left behind, we jolted on.

'Now we will stop for a piece of cake,' announced Alcibiades. 'It was made by my cook and it is something special.' He had talked of this cake once or twice, waiting eagerly for the moment when we would cut it. And strangely enough, it was the most perfect, sticky, golden sponge cake rich with eggs and the clarified butter which the catingueiros keep in bottles. A caviare of a cake, which was cut and cut again and passed between the passengers of the jeep and of the Rural, which had now caught us up. (Because of the dust clouds, vehicles must travel at some distance from each other, though in this car-less waste the problem seldom arises.)

'So you visited Colonel Mariano?' enquired Senhor Pedro.

'He's wealthy.' Alcibiades had, in fact, introduced the Colonel as the rich man of the region.

'The richest man in a land of beggars,' the old man had retorted.

As we drove, the land became progressively drier, the naked trees shining like bone under the sun.

'We are reaching the watershed,' announced Alcibiades. Six beautiful, pale donkeys cast black shadows on a sheet of cracked mud.

'This is the frontier of Piauí. And here the Padre's road begins.'

This was the first link with the outside world, opening the land to infinite possibilities.

'Until 1963, there was nothing but a mule track from here on, and no vehicle could pass. All our heavy supplies came from São Raimundo. For the rest, it was horseback – or donkey, the jeep of the sertão.'

'But how did you make the road with no machinery? What tools did they use?'

'Just picks and shovels, mattocks and machetes. The tools were supplied by the Fundação.'

'And how did they tackle the mato with the terrible thorns and the cactus?'

'The work is hard and there were accidents, but the men are used to the work of clearing. The catingueiro, like his animals, is tough. He has to be. The worst thing is the wood.'

He pointed to a gnarled trunk. 'We call that the blade-breaker because it is hard enough to smash a machete. After the ground is cleared all the tree stumps must be rooted out or burnt off level. And then the road surface must be cleared of rocks and the worst holes filled in.'

The jeep was tossing like a small boat on a rough sea. From time to time we would roll down the side of a riacho and, if the dry river bed was firm enough, take a rush at the other side. But in many cases the bed was sand and had to be crept across, and the opposite bank clawed up in four-wheel drive.

'We are no longer isolated now that we have the truck and our jeep,' said Alcibiades proudly. 'Why it was 1924 before the first car reached Teresina, the capital of our State, but such a thing was never even seen by most of the people here until a few years ago.'

'When the first Caravelle arrived at Teresina a crowd of two thousand rushed on to the tarmac shouting. The crew panicked and locked the doors until they saw that the people were kneeling and patting the wheels and kissing the paintwork. This was progress, you see. It was reported in *Manchete*,' said the Monsenhor, catching a sceptical glance from Alcibiades.

The caatinga stretched all round us, silvery and cinnamon with the wavering blue line of the Serra dos Dois Irmães on the horizon. As we twisted between the thorny walls a great bird, pale grey with long red legs, ran along the track before us, the tuft of feathers rising above its beak nodding anxiously at each backward glance.

'A seriema. Upá!' they cried, driving still faster as the poor creature ran.

'But why doesn't it step into the mato or fly away?' I asked.

'They run like that for miles, sometimes we even run them over,' replied the driver. It was like a nightmare – the poor bird sharing one's own foolishness, running through the sand, legs failing beneath the pounding heart, snatching terrified glances at the monster behind, unable to take the liberating move from the course marked out before it. Finally, with a flustered plunge, the heavy body rose slowly and, shaving the tops of the trees, fell into the scrub.

'Do they always behave like that?' I asked.

'They hate to fly,' replied Monsenhor Nestor, 'and sometimes after flying they die, or lie exhausted so that one can run into the mato and catch them. I had a pet once which became quite tame.'

'They're good to eat,' muttered the driver ominously. I couldn't help feeling that the jeep would bring in many a seriema as the dry season lengthened and food became scarce.

We had been driving for six hours and our eyes and limbs ached.

'Is it much further to the Fundação?' I enquired.

'We shall be in Curral Novo soon and then it is only nine kilometres,' replied Alcibiades. A few moments later we passed what looked like a deserted stable.

'The State school of Curral Novo,' said Alcibiades, and pointing to a small square building with blue shutters, 'my house.'

Hooting wildly, we drove through a wide space between a few small houses. In the middle stood a cross and a chapel. This was the village of Curral Novo with its ten families and the first shop we had seen on the whole journey. There were nine more kilometres to go.

A little nervously I tried to powder my nose and repair some of the ravages of the journey. This was an official visit. There would be an organised reception.

At this moment, a tall black figure, nearly naked, sprang from the mato and, like a human seriema, ran before the jeep glancing back in terror, eyes rolling, legs pounding the stony track. The driver hooted. Alcibiades leant out and called. But the poor creature ran on, fearing perhaps to be cornered among the thorns if he jumped aside, unaware that the beast in pursuit was itself tied to its track.

It was only after a mile or so that the poor fellow finally tumbled, exhausted, to one side, and even then he raised himself on one elbow to shake his fist as we passed.

'He's the brother of one of the pupils,' remarked Alcibiades.

The road was now wide enough for three vehicles to pass, the felled trees and brush laid back to each side in a swathe.

'What is happening here?' we asked.

'Padre Lira wanted to straighten the road a bit. It twisted too much, so he widened it a bit to take out the kinks,' we were told. This certainly gave a feeling of approach.

The road made a final sweep and the driver was blowing his

horn. We drove through a gate in a wire fence and there lay the Fundação, four buildings set on three sides of an empty square, white and tidy in the vast emptiness of the caatinga.

We skirted the left-hand building, turned the corner and drew up. A small crowd of people was waiting to greet us, led by Padre Lira. He introduced us formally to each of the men, who shook hands murmuring '*Muito prazer*'. This is the usual greeting exchanged in Brazil and corresponding to our 'How d'you do'.

One after another the women, from the four professoras and numerous mothers with babies in their arms to a jolly black-moustached woman in a black cotton dress, who turned out to be the wife of Senhor Pedro, embraced me. Not the formal *abraço*, which varies from a pat on the shoulder to a two-armed hug, nor the butterfly touch on the left and right cheek of the drawing rooms of Rio, but a solemn, biblical kiss and clasp of the hand.

14

WE had reached the Fundação and their first *festa* had begun. The four professoras showed us to our room, which was normally shared by two of them. To reach this we passed through a barely-furnished sitting room, cool after the burning heat outside, and on to a verandah which ran past the bedrooms to the dining room at the far end. A single enamel basin, perched on the verandah parapet, served for ablutions for the whole Fundação.

Pouring water from a tin into the basin, they offered us soap and towel while people stared in wonder. At first it was an embarrassment to clean one's teeth in public and spit onto the embryo garden below while onlookers watched to see if the

'Inglezes' were really like themselves. But the newly-installed W.C. was a blessing, like the shower which the Padre insisted we should use, in spite of the fact that every drop of water had to be brought to its tank on endless donkey-back journeys from the dwindling pool in the valley below.

It was difficult to discover how the Fundação, like the old woman in the shoe, could accommodate so many people – and indeed we never did solve the problem since there were only five bedrooms in all, and we were eighteen at table in the dining room, besides odd helpers.

Houses in the North-East owe their flexibility to the hammock, which may be hung anywhere, and to the rush mats which can be thrown on the floor to be used as beds. Simple hotel rooms are often furnished with only a table and some hooks for the hammocks which the guests bring with them. These make a comfortable bed, once one has the knack of lying diagonally to avoid a curve in the spine and provided that, in a chilly place like the caatinga at night, there is something warm to wrap oneself in. Hammocks come in all sizes, single, double and small ones for children.

We were already late and Padre Lorenz, a tall man with thick glasses and hair *en brosse*, who was limping after a fall from a horse, cut through all ceremony and ushered us into the small dining room where Kenneth and I, side by side as is the custom with man and wife in Brazil, were seated together with Padre Lira, Senhor Pedro, Monsenhor Nestor and Padre Lorenz. On the clean white tablecloth each glass was standing upside down because of the flies, and plates too were thoughtfully reversed.

We had expected frugality and hoped to lose a little weight, but this was the good season and a *festa*, and Brazilians usually have hearty appetites, so it was difficult to take small helpings. By some magic, abundant and excellent meals emerged from the earth-floored lean-to kitchen. There was chicken and pork and home-made sausage with mountains of rice and black beans, and even a small salad with precious tomatoes and shreds of sliced cabbage and onion.

'Take as much as you can. They want you to eat,' encouraged Padre Lorenz. 'They want to eat themselves. They will be disappointed if you don't.' Fortunately, his stage directions caused no embarrassment as they could be given in German which no one else understood.

Meals were served by the professoras who sat at the other table with Senhor Pedro's wife and family and the fiancé of the youngest professora, Rosinha, who had come to visit her and slung his hammock under a tree.

Having slept only three or four hours on the previous nights and with heads spinning from the long hot journey, we retired to our room for a rest, and a brief silence descended on the Fundação. Houses in the caatinga are built with open ceilings so that every last whisper of air can circulate. But every tiny sound can circulate too, and at first we found this trying, but we soon felt easy in the general climate of goodwill.

At four o'clock, tea was served by the housekeeper, Dona Ana, a small capable woman, and afterwards, Melita, a handsome dark-haired girl who was obviously the dominant character amongst the professoras, came to fetch us.

'Would you like to visit the huts?' she said.

Melita explained that the great problem, with a population so scattered, was that the distance from home to school was often too great. So the Padre offered outlying families a supply of roof tiles and timber if they would build themselves a hut on Fundação ground where the mother, with her children of school age or smaller, could stay during the term between May and November while the father and the other members of the family remained on their land.

So far, four families had accepted the offer and four little huts, the walls built of staves and open to the wind and the cold of the night, as well as transparent when lamplit, housed up to a dozen inhabitants each.

The first we visited was occupied by a plump, maternal

creature with a gipsy gaiety very unlike the other women. She met us at the entrance to a small patio fenced with staves.

'Come in,' she said. 'Welcome.'

Two daughters, pupils at the school but barefoot now and sparsely clothed, came forward to shake hands. A small chubby boy tottered naked on the earth floor. The hut was divided in two, rolled-up hammocks and mats hooked to the walls, the neat school uniforms hanging from a forked branch.

A beautiful apricot hand-tooled saddle hung over a rafter. It belonged, the woman explained, to an old man who had ridden in for the Concentração. Lifting a flap she showed us pouches for toilet things, flint and tinder and so on. Larger pockets beneath held a hammock and spare clothing.

'How many children does the Senhora have?' I asked.

'Eleven, but only seven of mine are here. Three more are living with me who belong to a friend,' she added beaming. Everything in the hut was neat and tidy. In the patio a tiny fire burned beneath a clay pot. Food for eleven? How was it possible to keep a healthy family in such a tiny space?

Following my glance the woman said, 'We make our own cooking pots. It is quite easy. You shape them with your hands. That one is iron,' she added proudly, pointing to a small black three-legged cauldron just like the souvenirs carved in bogwood which the Irish sell to tourists.

At each of the other huts we paid our call, the women welcoming us inside, though unlike the 'gipsy' clearly nervous of foreigners. At the fourth hut, the father of the family was in charge since the mother had taken the smallest child, who had an eye complaint, to hospital in São Raimundo. A year ago this would have been unthinkable and the child would probably have become blind. Once more we shook hands, uneasily, since trachoma is marked on our medical map as endemic in the North-East and we were not too sure what this implied.

'Each family makes its own huts with the materials we provide, and when all the children have passed through school, the hut is left for somebody else,' Melita explained. 'Of course these huts are very primitive and cold at night and we hope, when the money comes in, to make permanent dwellings which can be used by one family after another.'

For the women, who are often pregnant, this simple life is a release from drudgery at home and a wonderful chance of companionship and interest in the bustle of the school and the gossip of the kitchen.

Supper again was abundant and gay, Padre Lorenz limping round with a bottle of wine, which Padre Lira with a curious gesture of abnegation refused, choosing instead a glass of sticky syrup made from one of the wild fruits.

On the sandy ground outside the sitting room door we had noticed a huge pile of wood, the twisted limbs tinder dry.

'Come out to the fire,' said Padre Lira after supper.

While we were at table the bonfire had been lit. The cane rocking chairs which normally stood in the sitting room were arranged in a circle on the sand. The fire threw a great glow across the darkness and above stretched an infinite black vault where stars of a startling brilliance flashed each side of the pale swathe of the Milky Way.

One by one we of the 'high table' took our places, Padre Lira in his tropical cassock, Monsenhor Nestor wearing his usual grey flannel trousers, Padre Lorenz his sports shirt. Senhor Pedro, paunched and jolly, settled beside the neat form of Alcibiades.

There was a long silence broken by small cries and rustlings from the mato while gradually the lacy forms of the trees printed themselves onto the darkness like a slowly developing photograph.

'Well, Dona Peggie, so you're here. It seems like a dream. You like the Fundação? Is it what you expected?'

'Far more. It's a miracle. But there is so much I want to know. The Monsenhor and Seu Alcibiades have been your lightning conductors and answered our questions so patiently, but we must ask you a great deal too. How did you find the land? How did you start to build?'

It was now that we learnt of the early struggles and how Alcibiades had ridden through the caatinga searching for weeks and finally come upon the old woman in her hut. The Padre pointed to a tiled roof supported on four posts. The whole erection was not more than ten feet square.

'Her hut is a small piece of our history. Now it is used for preparing the *merendas*, the school meals which we give the children.'

'And what do you give them?'

'A porridge made of manioc flour or corn meal mixed with powdered milk or oil. About a third of the food comes from the School Meals Service and the rest is made up with food from Caritas. The children leave their homes without eating anything and many of them walk for miles, so they start the day with a merenda before lessons and have another at mid-day and a third before they leave for home. The children are completely changed since they have been regularly fed. Unfortunately, we can only provide for them during the term.'

'And how did everything begin?'

'Alcibiades will tell you. First, the mato had to be cleared.'

Since the compound and the building sites measured many hundreds of square yards, we realised what a daunting task this must have been. To us, the compound had seemed arid and defenceless beneath the burning sun, with only the twin rows of newly-planted saplings to give some relief to the eye, but to someone who had struggled all his life with rending thorns and tangled thickets such emptiness must seem luxurious.

Alcibiades pointed to a venerable tree lit by the glow from the fire.

'For the first six months I slept in a hammock beneath the branches. It was my home while we cleared the mato and worked on the buildings. And now Padre Lira wants to cut it down!'

It was strange that although the Padre called his uncle – a man of seventy – by his simple christian name, Alcibiades always referred to his nephew as 'Padre Lira'.

'You see that tree on the far side of the compound?' asked Alcibiades. The dim form was just discernible.

'That is the tree where Padre Lira said our first mass. That must never be cut down.'

The Padre smiled affectionately at his uncle, the slight cast in his left eye giving him an air of complicity.

The old man told how building materials were made on the spot or brought in on mule or donkey-back in the early days.

'But now that we have roads everything is changed. Last year we built 115 kilometres of road and this year we shall build more,' said the Padre, 'and soon I shall be able to visit every one of the chapels once a month, and we shall start other schools . . .' His eyes glowed in the firelight. 'If God wishes,' he added quietly.

'And how many children do you have here?' asked Kenneth.

'Eighty-three here and eighty-seven in Cacimbas. We shall go there tomorrow. It is the poorest place in the whole "parish", but the school is well attended.'

A great branch stirred in the fire and a golden shower of sparks startled a mongrel dog flattened in the sand.

'And the four professoras?'

'Melita and Rosinha teach "letras" [this meant elementary reading and writing and arithmetic] and Diva teaches embroidery by hand and Mariinha by machine. Conçeição was with us for the last two years, and now she has come back from her teacher training course to spend the holidays.' He signed to a quiet slender girl to move into the chair vacated by Senhor Pedro.

Dim figures stirred in the firelight. The professoras were grouped on the steps by the entrance door and Miguel, the odd-job man with his bare bony feet, faded shirt and battered leather hat, huddled by the fire.

'Miguel was a catcher of cattle on foot,' whispered Alcibiades. 'We found him here hungry and nearly naked. It is the lowliest job in a poor country where every man who handles cattle can ride. Now he sleeps on the kitchen floor and eats three times a day.'

15

THAT night the wind cut like a fine blade through the wooden shutters and pierced the house from end to end under the open roof. Somewhere beneath the rafters a dry cough rose and fell with the noise of a file. With our clothes piled on the bed for extra warmth I dozed and shivered and finally, at the first apprehension of dawn, rose and went out onto the verandah to wash in privacy.

The enveloping darkness slowly paled and an apricot flush marked the place where the sun would rise. Gradually the delicate shapes of naked branch and clustered cactus engraved themselves upon the emptiness. The cold water stung my face and arms and, once used, I poured it carefully into the hollow round one of the plants set in the bare earth below. Turning on a tap should never again be a thoughtless action, I resolved, though it is almost beyond a human being to preserve a sense of gratitude when a minor hardship is removed.

The small flowers in the earth below glowed with a rosy incandescence. Would they, I wondered, be able to gain a firm hold before the drought set in? Would the Fundação survive the hard times which must lie ahead?

The door next to ours opened and Dona Nilsa, pinned into her dusty black dress, padded barefoot onto the verandah, toothbrush in hand. Exchanging greetings, we stood for a moment side by side and arms on the parapet while the first rays of the sun touched us with a briefly welcome warmth.

'Coffee is at seven,' said Dona Nilsa. 'You must leave just afterwards to get to Cacimbas in time for the first *merenda*.'

Breakfast was abundant. A great bowl of curds was passed to us.

'Eat them,' advised Padre Lorenz. 'You need them for your intestines. The air is so dry here.'

Next came the plates of hard but savoury sausage, flakes of fried chicken, and the goat's milk cheese bought by Alcibiades. It was tainted for me by the memory of the flies, but we had to eat appreciatively to please the old man.

Instead of bread we were given slabs of a leathery, not unpleasant substance which is made of white, grainy manioc flour mixed with water and poured on to the hot stove. We ate this with eggs fried in oil. Finally the cook brought slabs of sweetmeat made from fruit collected in the mato.

The grey-streaked dawn had brought clouds, but the sky was so vast that they just scattered without obscuring the sun.

'If this were England I would have said it was going to rain,' I said to Alcibiades.

'It never rains at this time of the year,' he replied.

We piled into the jeep and set out for Cacimbas, branching off after Curral Novo onto a new road made by the Padre's men.

'Better put your dentures in your pocket,' advised Senhor Pedro, as he did so.

The driver, sun glasses pushed up on to his forehead, jumped the old Rural from rock to rock with canny expertise, taking the riachos by storm or stealth.

Alcibiades and Monsenhor Nestor were discussing Padre Lorenz's accident.

'The horse stumbled and Padre Lorenz leant forward to clutch at its neck. This is the signal for a gallop, for when the catingueiro is chasing a cow through the thickets he lies on the horse's back, leather hat first, sometimes with just one foot in the stirrup and the other leg hooked over the saddle and his whole body parallel with that of the horse, and zig-zags off after the animal. The Padre lost a stirrup and fell, and the horse stopped in its tracks and remained immovable. This they are trained to do, so that a man can jump down to rope a steer and find the animal just where he left it. The Padre had concussion, poor fellow, and when they arrived, there were the two of them as if carved from stone.'

We passed a stand of prickly pears. 'Those are used for fodder too,' said Alcibiades, 'and they have a reserve of water in the bulbous root which comes in handy in times of drought. The fruit can be eaten as well, though the prickles are dangerous to your fingers as well as your mouth.'

'Stop the car,' said the Monsenhor and he jumped out to pick a pale lily-like flower with slender, waisted petals and a spray of mauve stamens.

'A *mucambé*,' he said, handing it to me. 'The bark makes a wonderful expectorant.'

After another hour's jolting the horn was blowing once more and we breasted a rise and drew up before a couple of huts, solidly built of red clay beaten into a wattle framework.

Under the dark green shade of a juazeiro tree a hammock was slung beside a tethered donkey. The headman of the hamlet rose from the hammock, the women clustered round, and once again there was the ceremony of the welcoming embrace.

Three young professoras, until recently pupils at the Fundação, and as the Padre said, only a few months ahead of their pupils, shook hands in turn. Maria das Virgems, tall and handsome, was leaving to get married in the autumn; Zilma, dark and lively with a hint of negro blood, was wearing a yellow dress dotted with pearl beads, and Maria Nercy, who clearly had some native Indian ancestor, was dressed in scarlet. All three were wearing the sharply-pointed uplift bras which had recently swept Brazil, and all were smiling and eager to show off their pupils.

'It is time for the merenda,' said Padre Lira, and he led us

Padre Lira and Muriel on the terrace of our flat in Rio

At the Concentração: Alcibiades with the rolled-up Union Jack under his arm

The road to the Fundação, the first to be built by the Padre's men

Padre Lorenz in the caatinga

Catingueiros, leather-clad against the thorns of the mato

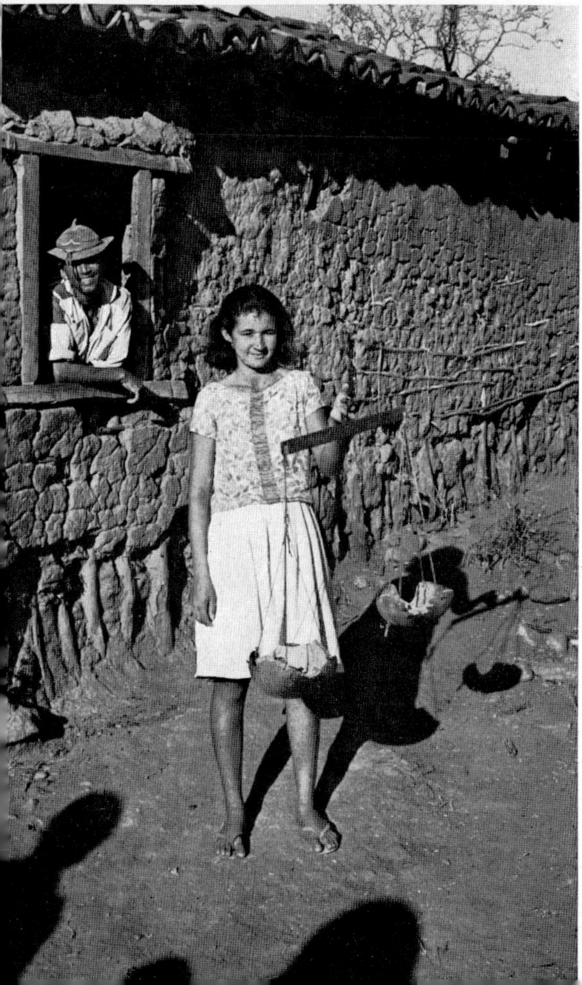

Tiago watches while Iracy shows us a balance made from armadillo shells

'Running water'. The donkey trots right into the kitchen with supplies from the riacho half a mile away

Sausage making. Raimunda washing entrails in a wooden dish

to a hut surrounded by a compound with a high wooden step-over at the entrace to keep out the pigs. Here the pupils, all dressed in clean school uniforms were thronging round a table beneath a canopy of branches while their plates were filled with gruel.

Any uniform works a curious transformation, and these children in their spotless clothes seemed like visitors to some primitive settlement beside their ragged mothers and their fathers, leather-hatted and lean amongst the tethered horses.

Hands were shaken, more embraces exchanged. Children were brought shyly to touch the English people.

'I never thought I should see an Inglez before I died,' said one old woman happily.

I was led to the kitchen and shown a bubbling cauldron with greyish, lumpy contents. In a small clay pot dark gobbets were simmering.

'Meat,' said a woman proudly. Today was a festa, the finest of the year.

'A chair for the Senhora,' she called, and I was sat in the shade of the overhanging roof in full view of the whole company, while woman after woman spoke to me, patted my shoulder, and felt the material of my cotton dress.

Padre Lorenz, meanwhile, was photographing as usual, laughing, gesticulating and crouching or straining on tip-toe.

'Where is the child who was bitten by a snake?' I asked.

A plump girl with heavy eyes was brought towards me, while the father described the accident.

'She was sleeping on the ground when a snake came into the house. [Since the floors are of earth, usually without a threshold, this can easily happen.] The cat began to play with the cobra. [In Brazil any snake is called a 'cobra'.] The snake in a fury struck it and then went on and bit the child in the neck,' he showed a small dark mark. 'It was two months before she could walk.'

The Padre bustled us off across the open ground to a small chapel, repaired about thirty years before, though now needing refurbishing, by the headman of the hamlet whose barrel-shaped tomb stood on the bare earth beside it.

We climbed some steps on to a small brick terrace and entered the windowless interior. Dazzled after the blazing light outside, we could just see rows of children perched on narrow wooden benches. In the corner, an ancient gramophone was wheezing out a tune.

The pupils rose to their feet while the Padre made a little speech. Now we had not known of the visit to Cacimbas and had only brought sweets for the children at the Fundação, so the Padre had suggested that the 7-lb bag of raisins which we had bought for his kitchen should be distributed at Cacimbas.

The raisins were poured into plates and each professora went round her group doling them into the outstretched hands. There was a pause as the children nibbled the fruit and then, one after another, the faces crumpled in disappointment.

'I don't like them,' said a little bright-eyed boy, and all but the most adventurous chirped 'Don't like them,' as the poor little professoras went round again with their plates collecting the sticky fruit.

'These are raisins – grapes. They are English. They are good,' said the Padre. 'Well, give them to the grown-ups.'

Hands stretched out from all around and the raisins disappeared fast. At this, the children started to call out, 'Give some to me,' but it was too late.

This dilapidated chapel, with its altar hidden by a ragged tarpaulin, is the only building in Cacimbas which can be used as a school, and since it is not large enough, the children must be taught in shifts. In order to write, they have to kneel on the floor and rest their exercise books on the benches.

A procession was being marshalled by Padre Lorenz. Three groups of children, each led by a professora, were to go down the chapel steps, round the open space beside it and up on to the rise by the kitchen while he took a ciné film.

'Now you must come and see the house where the professoras live,' said the Padre.

Behind the chapel stood a hovel, nothing but a single room, windowless and earth-floored, about nine feet square. There was no furniture. Three pairs of hooks carried the professoras' hammocks and three cheap suitcases held their clothes. A few oleographed piety cards were pinned to the mud wall as decoration.

Outside, under a brushwood awning, was a wooden table daubed with a thick layer of clay. On this, a tiny fire was burning and some gruel bubbling in a clay pot. The Padre pointed to a plastic basin and a rusty tin half filled with water underneath the table.

'That is the professoras' bathroom,' he said. 'For the rest, they have to use the mato.'

It was extraordinary to see these girls gay and prettily dressed, in spite of living cut off even from the tiny village of Curral Novo, except for an occasional excursion to mass there. Their only amusement was the ancient phonograph with its half dozen cracked records.

'These girls are very brave,' said the Padre. 'They are the real heroines. We need a proper school building with space for embroidery classes. We need desks and most of all, a house for the professoras.'

'What a wonderful place to save up for a trousseau,' muttered Padre Lorenz, and this seemed about the only advantage Cacimbas, in its present state, had to offer.

From the village we went with Padre Lorenz and Alcibiades to see the natural rock basin which had been cleared out and closed by a temporary dam so that it would hold the water from the rains.

Following a stony track we reached a deep pool surrounded by outcrops of rock.

'When the rains come, millions of litres of water run through the riachos cutting communications and tearing away the vegetation,' said Alcibiades. 'If we could only hold that water our problem would be solved. Here we must dynamite the rock to widen the pool, and raise the dam by a metre. There is still a fair supply of water even now, and when the reservoir at the Fundação dries up – I shall take you to see it this evening – we shall send the truck and fill our drums here, for as long as the supply will last.'

We were crossing the upper end of the rock face. Looking down into the greenish water I could see some small fish, but it was so much more appetising than the fetid water-hole on the Remanso road. Like every other scrap of water for human consumption this was carefully fenced.

As we talked, Padre Lorenz was busily photographing the cactus growing from the silvery rock face. Looped through the branches of a tall bush I found a string of dried blossoms like delicate carvings, honey-coloured on their wiry stems.

'Why, these would fetch pounds in London. Even in Brasilia they are selling dried flower arrangements at fancy prices. Perhaps one day you could start an industry . . .'

As we left, Maria Nercy handed us a bottle of the clarified butter which the catingueiros store and use for special dishes.

'My mother prepared this,' she said shyly.

Lunch at the Fundação was followed by a rest behind closed shutters and then each professora showed us her classroom, well-equipped and thronged with bright-eyed children in their pale blue and black uniforms.

'These children are extraordinarily intelligent and learn with such a will,' said Melita. In the silence of the sertão their minds had lain fallow and were eager and receptive.

We were shown the Padre's office, orderly and spare as one might expect, and a row of store rooms containing tools, equipment, medicines and a pile of Caritas food. Samples of thread and embroidery silks were filed in home-made boxes numbered to correspond with the stocks on the shelves.

Beneath the archway joining the two halves of the building a group of children, some quite small, were stitching away at their embroidery frames under the eye of the professora Diva, a birdlike little woman.

In a neighbouring room the professora Mariinha was supervising sixteen girls bent over treadle sewing-machines and doing elaborate embroidery, some with delicate drawn-thread insertions. A number of girls were making motifs of animals and flowers and nursery rhyme figures to sew on children's clothing. Samples of all the different designs were pasted on to a large sheet of cardboard.

'These are for you,' said Mariinha.

'They are beautifully made. How long do the girls take to learn?' I asked.

'I give myself up to a girl completely for the first week,' said Mariinha, a firm-featured woman in her late thirties. 'After that, she needs little help. When the girl has finished her course, she can take the sewing-machine home with her and continue working.'

Later, we saw a girl sitting in the middle of the earth floor on the only chair in her home, pedalling with bare feet, the exquisite tablecloth which she was embroidering bunched up out of the reach of the goats which frisked round the machine.

In the assembly hall, open to the mato on one side and the compound on the other, the crates of shoe-making machinery bought with the money from Cafod and Oxfam were being opened and the machines arranged ready for photographing.

At one end of the hall was a stage with a changing-room behind.

'Padre Lira says mass here,' said Melita who had joined us, 'and we have dances and meetings.' It was clear that this simple building fulfilled all the needs of a social centre.

As we talked, a flock of vivid green and yellow parakeets fluttered through the trees uttering small cries. These little birds are easy to tame and, once they are accustomed to human company, will roam freely round the house without flying away.

'Would you like to see our reservoir?' asked Alcibiades.

We crossed the compound and set off down a stony lane beyond the wire fence. In a small valley at the end of the track we came on a series of unfinished excavations. Opening a gate in the fence Alcibiades showed us a basin cut in what looked like solid rock.

'This was a great disappointment to us. We hoped that the rock would hold water, but it has proved spongy and porous. Even the earth is better.' We crossed the piled-up soil to two smaller excavations. In each, was a quantity of brownish water with drifts of algae floating on the surface.

'This is our drinking water. It is slowly seeping away, but with luck it may last us till September. After that, we must send the truck to Cacimbas until the reservoir there is exhausted too.'

Engineer Farias had proposed that the three pits should be joined to form a single reservoir with sloping sides, so that the whole interior could be lined with concrete slabs cast on the spot and joined with strips of asphalt to give elasticity. The finished reservoir would hold about one and a half million litres, sufficient for the Fundação's needs in a year of normal rainfall.

Local labour was not sufficiently skilled for the work, but the Padre was in touch with a gang in São Raimundo who had the necessary experience to carry out the job. But unless the money needed to build the reservoirs was secured in time to complete the work before the next rain, the whole neighbourhood would face another long dry season with only bitter, brackish water for drinking and almost none for washing.

As we walked up the steep little track a thin woman with a rusty tin of water balanced on her head, hurried after us.

'The Senhores live in England?' she asked.

'We live in Rio,' we replied. 'Where does the Senhora live?'

'I am a Paulista,' she replied proudly, as if all the bright lights shone behind her. 'This is a dead end.'

'She probably comes from some God-forsaken part of the State of São Paulo which is nearly as bad as here,' Alcibiades commented later.

In a corner of the compound Alcibiades showed us the site for the shoe factory.

'The building will have a flat roof which will drain into a cistern and supply the kitchen with sweet water. And when we have our generator we shall be able to pump it into a tank on the roof.'

Two cows stood in a small enclosure, one a pale zebu and the other deep brown. Two calves frisked outside beneath the umburana tree.

'The brown cow belongs to the Fundação. The other has been lent to us for the festas. They are both good. The brown cow gives five litres of milk a day.' This is a tiny output compared to an English dairy cow.

'Now we are going to distribute the clothes which you brought. The professoras have assembled our people in the dining room. Come and see.'

The sacks of clothes had been opened and everything was there, neatly folded and laid out on the tables. One by one, as they were called, each person stepped forward and chose what they most wanted. Perhaps they had come to some sort of agreement beforehand. Certainly there was no grabbing nor envious looks, just quiet contentment.

'Dona Peggie, I have a favour to ask,' said Alcibiades, pointing to one of my Marks & Spencer cardigans. 'Would you allow me to have that? It would be wonderful to wear in bed on a cold night.'

Outside in the compound there was an air of excitement. In the morning a man had cut up the carcases of two steers – a meat which is not very often eaten as the beasts are too valuable – and hung them, mantled with flies, from the beams of the hut where the children's merenda was made.

'Come and see the kitchen,' said Padre Lorenz. We walked in at the open end of the lean-to. A brick ledge running round the walls served as a working counter rather in the modern manner. Near the door stood a wood-burning stove. On ropes like washing lines hung translucent coils of inflated pig's guts and an old woman was busy stuffing others with the chopped bits and pieces which make up the local sausage.

Another woman was pounding coffee beans in a huge wooden mortar using a pestle four feet long, while Raimunda the cook, crouched over a hand-hewn wooden dish, was washing something ambiguous and bloody. Flies were everywhere. Amongst the dingy tins on the shelf the alarm clock stood out with startling modernity. It was difficult to understand how excellent meals for all of us could be produced with such equipment.

Behind the kitchen was a table-garden. Here the precious onions, beetroots and even a few tomatoes were coaxed into growth. Near at hand, a magnificent ten-foot mandacarú cactus, its abundant spikes branching out with perfect symmetry, held all the washing as efficiently as the gadgets advertised in women's magazines.

Amongst all this, a tame green parakeet hopped and chirruped, climbing on to any outstretched hand and pulling himself up by grasping mouthfuls of flesh in his tiny beak.

'There will be no bonfire tonight,' said the Padre. 'Tomorrow is the Concentração and we shall all go early to bed.'

After supper we sat in our rocking chairs while the sun sank fiery behind the caatinga and the horizon, like a lemon-sprinkled oyster, shrank at the first touch of gathering dark. As the chill of night fell from the clear sky a comforting warmth, acrid with the pungency of last night's ashes, rose from the baked earth.

Here in the sertão one was conscious of the wide surface of the globe, slowly turning. Tiny night cries carried through the clear air to give the sensation of heightened hearing. Sight too was sharpened, and as we rocked slowly, faces to the sky, we watched a satellite making its rounds, returning at regular intervals, having circled the whole globe between each appearance. The lights of the city blind one to so many marvels, even to the slow rhythms of the moon.

At nine o'clock we were all in bed. 'Work will begin at dawn tomorrow,' said the Padre. 'People are riding in from all over the "parish" for the Concentração. We are expecting about three hundred horsemen. Some have already been two days on the way. They are gathering in two groups and will spend the night in the mato.' He pointed east and west. 'They are there now, sleeping.'

'What do they sleep on?' I enquired.

'On the ground. Or some have hammocks in their saddle-bags. They don't worry. The earth is dry and at this time of year it never rains. They will light fires.'

It was strange to think of this host silently gathering in the scrub, lying on the hard ground in the knife-cold air.

16

THE hands of our travelling clock showed 5 a.m. in a faint glow. I crept to the window and pushed open the shutters. Under a black sky lit by huge stars figures were hurrying here and there with lamps. Already paper chains were hung along the face of each building between groups of paper pennants.

Padre Lira, in his pale robes, stood directing Miguel and the boy as they hoisted flags on masts which had been fixed in the four concreted blocks in front of the school building. First the Brazilian, and then the flag of the Fundação with its single flower on a bare black branch. At the far end was a flag which I took to be that of the State of Piauí and on the fourth mast, a splendid Union Jack.

I washed on the empty verandah. The plants were already watered, each in its nest. After dressing, I roused Kenneth. The Padre, with serene authority, was still issuing commands. Professoras carrying tablecloths and bundles of plates crossed and re-crossed the wide compound between the assembly hall and the kitchen. Dona Nilsa, short arms stretched out penguin-wise in the fat woman's gait, waddled helpfully after them.

Unbolting the outer door we stepped into the chill. Against the first faint flush of the horizon the black tracery of the caatinga slowly emerged. Birds were crying in a frenzy of territorial aggression. It seemed that even the whole wide sertão was not sufficient for peaceful cohabitation.

Melita, handsome and intent, brought steaming cafezinhos as Alcibiades, in khaki drill and leather hat, rode up on a skewbald pony. As the first rays of the sun shone on the flags I took a picture. A moment more and the sun had burst over the horizon.

Each of the professoras was wearing a new and brilliant dress. Miguel was magnificent in a green shirt fluttering to meet the trousers slung low on his long legs. From the family huts came curls of smoke and small naked bodies.

Dona Ana came to call us to breakfast. 'You must eat a lot,' she commanded. 'This is a big day.'

By nine o'clock the sun was blazing remorselessly and everyone keeping as far as possible to the rim of shadow beneath the eaves of the buildings. Padre Lorenz with his photographic team – Rosinha carrying a parasol to shade his lens from the sun and her fiancé loaded with spare cameras like a caddy at a golf tournament, loped in and out of the Fundação enclosure.

'At ten o'clock Alcibiades will muster the horsemen and ride into the compound at their head. No one can remember when so many horsemen assembled round here.'

'How will you feed them?' I asked.

'That is arranged,' replied the Padre calmly.

'And the horses?'

'They will find something to eat on their way home,' he replied.

Meanwhile the great empty space outside the wire fence had been filling with horsemen, streaming in from the approach road and along a track leading from the opposite direction. On small wiry mounts, all like their masters lean and resistant, the men made for the shade of the few trees where the beasts were tethered, heads to the centre. Many a man had a wife on the pillion or a child in his arms. Some of the older women were riding side-saddle, their feet slapping against the horse's flanks. In a patch of shade, a horsewoman gave her baby the breast.

At a discreet distance away in the scrub the girls pulled off the trousers which some wore beneath their cotton frocks. Only the most daring would be seen in slacks without a dress on top.

One handsome man, Seu Pericles, with a pointed silver beard and flashing eyes, circled the bushes where the girls were changing. Young men whipped their horses into a gallop and rushed with loud cries amongst the admiring crowd.

Children were running everywhere. The plump naked baby of the 'gipsy' mother was being squeezed into tight little pants and socks. Men were pulling on clean shirts, carefully ironed but creased from hours in the saddle-bags.

Every man wore a leather hat moulded to his own personality. These hats, which may be of simple hide with lines of stitching, or trimmed with fine bands of scarlet, turquoise and green leather, are a necessary part of the catingueiro's equipment. Day by day they protect him from the scorching sun and save him from a scalping when he rides after the cattle. To keep the hat in place against the wind it is fitted with a strap which hangs across the forehead and another which crosses the back of the neck. These straps are threaded through the crown to emerge at either side, cut into a handful of long fringes. By pulling on the fringe, the straps can be regulated to hold the hats in any position. This basic shape is then adapted by each man to his fancy. Some wear the brim turned up in front; others in a tricorne. With age and the gradual accretion of dust and grease, each hat acquires an individual character.

The Padre sent a small boy to summon us to the foot of the flagstaffs.

'Where did you get that beautiful Union Jack?' we asked.

'Dona Ana made it, as well as the one you will see hung above the platform in the assembly hall.' The flag measured a good four feet across.

'Are they all right?'

I nodded. It would have been churlish to mention that all the white bands should not have been of equal thickness. In any case, I have never been too sure of the design myself.

'We found a picture of the flag in a magazine,' he explained.

'And what is the one next to it?'

'That is the flag of the State of Piauí,' he confirmed. 'Wait here a moment.'

He hurried into his office and emerged with a parcel which he handed to Kenneth. 'This is for you. You are to wear it for the Concentração.'

It was a leather hat. A great untamed cartwheel of raw-hide intricately decorated with strips of coloured leather. The gift was touching and of great value.

Alcibiades on his little horse was galloping in and out of the entrance gate. He had a thin brown paper parcel under his arm. The Padre looked at his watch and issued some commands.

'You will stand beside me in front of the flagstaffs,' he ordered us.

'May we go a little nearer to take photographs as the men ride in?' we asked. Rather reluctantly he agreed and we hurried to catch the scene as the first men came through the gate.

By the time we returned to our posts most of the riders were massing at the far end of the compound, Alcibiades riding up and down in front of them, waving his arms in a martial manner.

At a sign from the Padre, Alcibiades whipped the brown paper from the parcel and, unfurling a Union Jack, charged forward at the head of the horsemen, right across the compound and up to the flagstaff. It was a splendid sight, for all the oddness of the mounts.

The ceremony over, little groups gathered to chat in the unhurried way of people who rarely meet their neighbours and are unused to company. In each small patch of shade men dropped to their heels and squatted in the easy pose of those who seldom find a chair to relax in.

Seu José, as the senior citizen of Curral Novo, had brought us a gift. This consisted of the de luxe version of the local substitute for a box of matches. Inside a linen pouch trimmed with pink baubles and bands of blue and green felt was a cow's horn holding cotton fibre. From the wide end of the horn a piece of rough iron dangled on a strip of raw-hide. A handful of flint chips completed the equipment. This primitive source of fire is used by all the local catingueiros, since to buy matches would be an unthinkable waste of capital.

Now the professoras were appearing with steaming dishes and the first shift of people sat down to tables laid in the assembly hall. Chairs for the 'establishment' were set on the stage. From here, the Monsenhor, Dona Nilsa and her husband, ourselves and an occasional dignitary like the *vereador*, or headman, of Curral Novo, himself illiterate but nevertheless of local importance, sat and watched. Padre Lorenz with his photographic team moved tirelessly from group to group saying, '*So, so. Das ist gut*', as he persuaded a shy face to turn towards him.

Places were neatly laid on the white tablecloth with plate, glass, knife, fork and spoon.

'The Padre knows how to organise,' observed Dona Nilsa. 'He has hundreds of plates and glasses and everything to go with them which were given him in São Paulo. They are kept in the store room.'

Each of the professoras, neat and fresh in spite of the heat, was serving a group of tables with stew, sausage and black beans, rice and toasted manioc flour to mop up the juice. This was a feast.

Gravely the catingueiros sat down to their meal, though most of them had never seen a table laid before. With perfect dignity they ate their food and then rose to allow another shift to replace them. Normally, any sort of country gathering in

Brazil is an excuse for drinking quantities of cachaça, but out of respect for the Padre, not a flask was seen.

'We expected to feed three hundred,' said the Padre, 'but with all the pupils we have nearly five hundred. People have come in from all over the country.'

'But how will you manage?' I thought of the small kitchen with its one wood-burning stove and primitive equipment.

'It will be all right,' the Padre replied with complete confidence.

One after another, the sittings came and went and the plates vanished, carried across the burning compound to return clean in a few minutes. Finally, it was our turn and we were served with the same meal by the unruffled professoras. Later, the Padre told me that until he decreed that broken crockery must be paid for, losses had been heavy, though now they had diminished considerably. I thought of the dusty little donkey trotting with his kegs backwards and forwards to the riacho and wondered how sufficient water could be accumulated to cook that monster meal and to wash the endless dishes, and afterwards the towels used to dry them.

Quickly the tables were cleared away and we returned to the platform. There was to be a quadrilha. Melita, in charge as usual, had put on a black dress with white polka dots and frills and, to the hoarse music of the old gramophone, she drilled the children through the complicated measures – twenty-four figures climaxing in the 'caracol', or snail, whose apparently inextricable knot unrolled smoothly. What started as a Portuguese court dance has become, in Brazil, a burlesque and the dancers, their faces painted like dolls, the girls dressed up as boys, wear bright patchwork clothes.

From time to time, Melita made an imperious gesture towards the platform.

'Seu Padre, that record is not suitable,' she called, obliging him to change the rhythm with an apologetic little smile.

By the time the quadrilha was over, guests from the more remote areas. already changed into their dusty travel clothes with sleepy babies bundled on the crupper, were riding away. We had been up since five, but they had slept rough and ridden for days through the mato.

It had been a wonderful event, something between Trooping the Colour and Sports Day at school. There had been a few small disappointments. Many people were unable to understand why photographs could not be seen as soon as they who were taken. Others came to ask us for a mule or a sack of flour had to be told that all good things were obtained and shared out by the Padre.

Dance music with a tireless beat was now coming from an accordion and a drum which played on and on without a single pause as the afternoon progressed. A few couples, all either engaged or married to each other, were gyrating solemnly. The edge of the floor was lined with people watching and listening.

'Where do they learn to dance?' I asked Monsenhor Nestor.

'They copy each other,' he replied.

'But there are not many couples dancing.'

'Most fathers would not allow their daughters to dance with a man who was not her betrothed. Why, if a young man and a girl went away as far as the kitchen,' he pointed across the compound, 'and stayed away for as much as quarter of an hour, the father would insist on their getting married. If the young man refused, he might well be shot.'

'Does the mother have nothing to say?'

'Nothing. Women of that generation simply don't count. Now things will be different. If a young couple want to get married and the father disapproves, then they must have a *quema*. This means that they must go secretly to the priest and get married. When they return home, the father may beat the girl, but he usually accepts the situation. It is better than dishonour.'

When we got up from a brief rest at seven, the beat of the drum had finally stopped. The last horse was saddled and a jeep from Remanso, painted with bunches of flowers and the slogan 'Two hearts with but a single thought' in large white letters, had bumped away down the road.

'What a wonderful day!' we said as our chairs rocked slowly under the stars.

'Not a plate broken,' replied the Padre.

17

NEXT morning, everyone sat down to a large breakfast at eight, wearing their best clothes. Monsenhor Nestor had discarded his flannel trousers and open shirt and was wearing a tropical cassock. Dona Nilsa was dressed as usual in black, though this time the tight garment was made of artificial silk. The professoras had fished yet other flowery numbers out of their marvellously contrived wardrobes.

The Fundação truck was filling with children in freshly-laundered uniforms and the first jeep-load setting off for Curral Novo.

'The chapel was a ruin until Padre Lira came,' the Monsenhor told us. 'He mended the roof and cleaned it up and painted the walls.'

'The money for the altar furniture and repairs came from Dona Muriel,' added the Padre.

Just as we were leaving, Conceição, always thoughtful and kind, came up with a white mantilla, neatly folded.

'For you to wear, Dona Peggie,' she said.

When we reached the chapel the children were already sitting on benches inside, with the professoras pacing the aisles. We were led up the centre to two thrones in the chancel, beside the altar, each with a cushion trimmed with red and blue frills. The white mantilla sheltered me with a sense of ceremony combined with a comforting feeling of anonymity.

On the altar the Union Jack was spread and behind it the

scarlet plastic poinsettias which I had brought, thinking they might be useful at Christmas in a place so devoid of colour. On the altar, which was set basilica-wise to face the people, was a tall case with some wires trailing from it. Two little boys in white pinnies sat motionless at the foot of the altar steps.

With the inexpert help of another little boy, both the Monsenhor and the Padre were vested. Older people and the parents of the pupils filled the back of the chapel and overflowed into the space outside.

If we felt a little lost, so also did some of the congregation to whom mass was still something rather strange, as well as Monsenhor Nestor, who was frankly bothered at coping with a service in the vernacular. Leaflets and manuals are slow to reach the back country, and he is now a headmaster, not a working priest.

So there was a welcome feeling of communal uncertainty, that we were all doing something a little unfamiliar together, and doing our best.

At one point in the service, Padre Lira advanced towards Kenneth with a silver ewer from which he poured water into a silver bowl.

'You will wash the hands of the Monsenhor,' he murmured. To me, he handed a towel. 'And you, Dona Peggie, will dry his hands.'

We wondered whether this custom derived from the regions where the all-powerful landlord had been made, publicly, to perform an act of service and acknowledge the supremacy of the Church.

The Monsenhor's sermon was short and sensible, though delivered in a charmingly formal manner. Now we could see the point of the case with its wires. Padre Lira, who as a small boy would have loved to play with trains, has a great feeling for gadgets and he had decided to make a recording of this special service.

Later, at supper, the sermon was played over, the Monsenhor clucking with pleasure when complimented on his oratory and saying, 'Quite spontaneous, you know. I always say just what comes into my head' – an interesting reversal of normal public-speaking where people usually struggle to make a prepared speech sound natural.

When mass was over, the children piled back into the truck and the professoras rode off in the jeep, after more photographs by Padre Lorenz.

Accompanied by Alcibiades and Senhor Pedro we started on a round of visits. First we entered the house of João João. Like all the houses in the area it had the open roof, but was divided between front and back by a white-washed masonry arch of a curious form. The roof of the house sloped out at the back to cover half the kitchen and was separated from the rest of the roof, which was pitched the opposite way, by a valley gutter. Where the slopes of the two roofs met, headroom was under five feet. The result was that passing from one side of the kitchen to another one had to duck between the supporting uprights. This inconvenience was amply repaid by the precious rainwater collected from the gutter into a small cistern.

Next we visited a 'poor man's' house, just two tiny rooms with a few hooks in the wall for hammocks. Black beans to last until the next harvest lay piled in one corner. In another, cotton which had been grown in the garden was stuffed into sacks ready for transport to Petrolina. The seeds, they told us, were made into oil that could be used in aeroplane engines.

'They are good for mothers after childbirth,' insisted an old woman, as if this were a much more important use. Certainly to her, the annual birth was more significant than an aeroplane she had never seen.

The garden, though small, was lovingly cared for and, seeing my interest, the women ran and broke off leaves which they crushed between their fingers for me to smell. Not too sure of the names, they nevertheless knew the use of every plant.

It is only recently that any of them ever saw medicine in a package or a labelled bottle. Before this, every remedy was gathered from the garden or the mato.

Since I admired the ingenious uses to which they had put gourds of various sizes the women hurried to offer me one of the largest. When Alcibiades pointed out that this would prove awkward to carry home, they hunted until they found a perfectly shaped miniature about an inch and a half long. On an inside wall hung a branding iron for cattle and an old saddle, worn but nevertheless a treasure in a country where many people ride on a folded rag rug.

Crossing the wide empty space in the middle of the village we came to the shop of Seu José. Fearing that the Padre's roads would slash his profits he had at first been a bitter opponent of all the new developments. Now he was perhaps beginning to realise that as the area became more prosperous people would have money to spend in his store and that the Padre might in the end make him a fortune.

So we were greeted with a rather wary smile as we entered the windowless rank-smelling shop and Seu José's narrow eyes assessed the unlikelihood of our buying any of his dusty plastic trifles or garish sweets. However, conscious of his position as the rich man of Curral Novo, he was prepared to do the honours.

So we shook hands with his wife and daughters and vague female relations and drank a glass of cachaça. Then Monsenhor Nestor spotted the skin of a wild cat hanging on a nail, stiff from unskilled curing.

'I will give that to the Senhores. How much?' said the Monsenhor grandly.

'Six contos,' replied Seu José. This was then about a pound and a lot of money in that part of the world. The situation was acutely embarrassing. This seemed a stiff price for a small cat skin and one feared that Seu José might be recouping himself for his offering to us, but we could not easily refuse the Monsenhor's gift nor appear to doubt his willingness to pay.

So I was obliged to plead a misplaced sympathy for the wild cat and decline the offer on a question of principle.

Afterwards we were told that the skin of an 'onça' is regarded as an article of luxury and that the price was not excessive. Now onça, like so many names in Brazil, is a vague term and can refer to a leopard, an ocelot or a jaguar – in fact anything cat-like which doesn't drink milk out of a saucer; but my informant knew the size of our creature and was unshakable in his opinion.

The Brazilians love giving presents. Luckily we had brought something for everyone and, apart from the fiasco at Cacimbas, were only once at a loss, and this unfortunately in the case of the Monsenhor whose presence we had not expected. This, however, we were able to remedy by sending a parcel of his favourite cigars to Remanso.

'You see that satchel there,' the Monsenhor pointed to a small wooden box on a leather strap. 'I used to take one like that to school every day.' Priests, like so many men whose sexual appetites have not been over-indulged, often seem to maintain a refreshing contact with their own youth.

The women of the family led us from the shop into the house. This was the most spacious we had seen, and the floors were tiled. We were invited to sit on hard chairs round a table with a chenille cloth, and were shown a statue of a cow and a bull made of the cheap glue-smelling substance of which fair-ground prizes are so often composed, both painted blood red.

'He and she,' observed the youngest daughter.

A few trade calendars and vases of plastic flowers on doilies completed what was for Curral Novo the acme of gracious living.

But it was outside the house that the real luxury lay. Beside the back door a cement tank had been recently built and when the iron cover was lifted we were shown water, two metres deep and glistening yellow-green in a shaft of light.

'That's what the Padre should do,' said Kenneth. 'If only

he could build a catchment cistern beside each building at the Fundação.'

'It is too expensive even to buy the guttering,' said Alcibiades. 'But we shall use the flat roof of the shoe factory.'

The garden contained another luxury, a large orange tree laden with fruit, the only one for many miles. And there were clumps of 'you-and-me', a thorny silver plant with coral flowers, and 'mother-in-law's tongue', the sharp yellow and green spears of which are now so successfully imitated in plastic.

As we left the shop a couple of men, already with half a dozen cachaças inside them, were careering their tiny mounts up and down in a two-man rodeo. We were amused by their antics, but the Monsenhor looked tolerantly disapproving.

'Now you must see the State school of Curral Novo,' said Alcibiades and we piled into the Rural and rode to the other end of the village, a distance of about a hundred yards.

A forlorn building stood behind a wire fence.

'This school was built in the time of President Dutra, thirty years ago. Since then, until Padre Lira arrived, it was used to shelter goats. One side was supposed to be a school room and the other, a dwelling for the teacher, very nice with a separate kitchen.'

In effect, the kitchen was merely a space partitioned off, with neither water nor light, nor any cooking facilities but a large stone on which to make a fire.

'They kept the goats in the teacher's side too and now she has to live in Seu José's house and her whole month's wages scarcely pay his bill.'

Considering that her pay only amounted to £1.50 a month, one could not maintain that Seu José's bill was exhorbitant.

When the Padre set up the Fundação, he insisted that the State school of Curral Novo should be re-opened. The goats were chased out, the building swept, and an untrained teacher was finally found.

The teacher welcomed us as we pushed open the rickety

door into the schoolroom. It was completely empty but for a table lent, as Alcibiades told us, by the Fundação.

'I have ninety pupils to teach and look at this . . . When the children have to write they kneel with their exercise books in front of them on the rough brick. But for Padre Lira we should not even have had pencils and paper. None have been sent us by the authorities.'

'When I went to Teresina to fetch the school books for the Fundação,' interrupted Alcibiades, 'I offered to take with me the exercise books for Curral Novo. The official told me to mind my own business and take what was my due. I replied that if he preferred to do without free transport that was his affair. That's how they treat the South-East of Piauí – and the man had a pile of books reaching almost to the ceiling. Now you must see my house.'

Across the way stood a small white building with two shuttered windows and a blue front door which opened straight into an austere room with the usual hooks for hammocks.

'This hammock is made from the fibre of the *caroá* – the plant with spear-shaped leaves which I showed you on the way, and the rope is twisted from the hair from a cow's tail. Take it – a *lembrança* – I can get another.'

Lembranças, or keepsakes, are very important to Brazilians and cover all sorts of presents and mementos from a picture postcard to a lock of hair. The expression is also used for 'greetings' at the end of a letter.

Alcibiades led us through a further door into a wide verandah. Beyond it, an extension at right angles to the house was almost completed.

'I am building in the style of the caatinga. It is ideal for our climate. Here is the bathroom and there the toilet. Except for the Fundação, these are the only ones within a two-day ride in any direction.'

When the extension was complete, the cottage would become a well-equipped small house with the textural charm of the open roof and the windows framing the grisaille of the caatinga.

'Padre Lira is going to take this house,' said Alcibiades, happy in his ambivalent role of indulgent uncle and respectful lieutenant. Later, we heard that the Padre planned to set up an embroidery school there for the women of the village while Alcibiades, presumably, would have to hang his hammock elsewhere, perhaps under another umbuzeiro tree.

'Look, Dona Peggie,' said Monsenhor Nestor, 'the roof tiles are supported on staves cut from the facheiro. The tiles are a mixture of clay and cow dung. The bricks were made here too. Only the windows and doors came from São Raimundo.'

At lunch we discussed our journey back, which had been planned for next morning.

'The aeroplane doesn't fly until two o'clock on Sunday. You needn't go back to Petrolina tomorrow,' said the Padre.

'But we don't want to abuse your hospitality . . .'

'Please stay. There are still so many things to show you. And Padre Lorenz will stay too, then you can all go back with Monsenhor Nestor on Sunday.'

We were delighted to accept, as long as we were making no unwelcome inroads on their supplies of food and water, but Padre Lorenz, our infallible guide in matters of etiquette and the domestic situation, assured us that all was well.

That afternoon we set out in the jeep to visit a few of the houses scattered in the mato and to see some land which had been bought for the Fundação three years before. Here, the Padre was planning to grow some pilot crops with a view to discovering what would survive the harsh conditions. The new land was covered with scrub and not only would this have to be grubbed up, in all its writhing thorny resistance, but until money could be found for wire, each plantation would have to be laboriously fenced.

In spite of the dryness, the mato is peopled with flitting birds. Small scaley doves, each of their white body feathers edged with black to look like the scales on a Chinese paper fish, call like quails. The concliz bird, black and fiery orange, sings with a fine powerful voice, while the tem-tem lies silent on the ground. The sleeper bird, yellow-collared and red-bearded above its glossy black plumage, sits motionless and dreaming until startled, when it flies away crying 'turüi, turüi'. High above, a hawk-like bird of prey which will devour lambs and kids hovers threateningly.

The jeep drew up before a wattle-and-daub cabin.

'The house of Tiago,' announced Alcibiades as a handsome, humorous man with leather hat jauntily cocked, stepped out to welcome us. Tiago's eldest daughter, Iracy, a pretty girl of fifteen who plans to become a professora, showed us the two rooms where the family lived. In one, Tiago's leather jacket and chaps were hanging beside his gun, which was used to shoot game and the plump prairie rats which are so welcome in the lean months.

Tiago showed us a balance made from the shell of two armadillos. These were strung from a cross-piece by cords made from the fibre of the caroá. I was charmed by the ingenuity of the catingueiros. As prosperity increases, plastics will inevitably replace the natural fibres, woods and clay, of the caatinga for domestic use, but the old skills, one hopes, will be channelled into some creative source of income.

Like all the houses in the area, Tiago's had a floor of earth and a window which was just a hole in the wall, but there, beside the hand-made clay pots and the heap of gourds and dried beans in the corner, stood a treadle sewing-machine which Iracy had brought home on finishing her embroidery course.

'If the girl fails to pay off her machine during the first year, the price rises by twenty per cent,' said Alcibiades. This is a powerful incentive to repay quickly and release money for the purchase of other machines, and the idea might well be copied elsewhere.

As Padre Lorenz was taking our photographs with Tiago's

family the debonair bearded Pericles galloped up and insisted on being included in the picture.

The next house we visited had a wide earth-floored verandah facing into the long rays of the afternoon sun. Again we had a gracious welcome and were led through the two rooms which housed the family, to the open-air kitchen at the back. Two goat skins were pegged out to dry like giant furry butterflies. These represented, now that the road was open, sugar, salt and coffee for many months.

Visiting in the caatinga one marvels at the size of the dwellings which shelter abundant families. A room fulfils its primary function as a shelter from the elements. Everything is pared down to a minimum. Each object has an essential function and there is no confusion. Litter is unknown. It is only from the remorseless indestructible packaging of the civilised world, which grows more resistant as its use becomes more transitory, that squalor is born.

'To visit the next house I am afraid we shall have to walk,' said Alcibiades as we set off along the stony track. 'There is the riacho.'

He pointed to some shallow pools set in a lush fringe of grass. The blue sky shimmered on the water, soothing one's smarting eyes.

'Can that water really be salt?' I asked.

'Salt and bitter too. It kills vegetables and flowers. That tough grass is planted in the riacho as fodder for the dry months. Nothing else will grow there.'

A donkey passed followed by a small boy, its forked wooden panniers loaded high with wood. A few minutes more, and we reached a hut, windowless and with a single door. The hut, with the beaten earth surrounding it and a single withered tree, was enclosed by a fence of twisted branches. At the entrance, a number of boughs were laid transversely to prevent the passage of pigs and small children.

From the figures clustered beneath the projecting roof a woman rose and came forward to welcome us with a beautiful gesture. Thin but serene, in her faded cotton frock, she pointed to the children scrambling round her. 'A poor man's house,' she smiled, 'but we have ten children.'

'The children are your riches, Senhora,' I replied according to convention.

In many places the clay daub had crumbled away until the house appeared too frail to stand, and the two rooms were so small that one wondered how twelve bodies could lie down to sleep, even though some were in hammocks and others on the floor.

Out in the yard a naked baby tottered around followed by a thin brindled dog which licked it kindly each time it fell. It is curious that while the rich girls of Copacabana spend a large part of the day clad only in a bikini, modesty compels the mothers of the caatinga to cover up their daughters, with the result that there is often not enough material left to clothe the smaller children.

Three of the children from this home were pupils at the Fundação. Out of school hours, their clothes were patched and faded. The father of the family led us round to the back of the house. On the wall were slung three hollow tree trunks daubed with clay.

'Those are nests of the *orópa*, or wild bee,' explained Alcibiades. 'It is only in the last two years that they have reached us from the South. Our water may be growing more saline, but we have at least the blessing of the honey. Each nest yields about three litres.'

This particular blessing is regarded with apprehension in the more prosperous parts of Brazil, and I have a newspaper cutting headlined, 'Wild Bees Kill 48 Birds and 1 Politician'. The writer explains that forty chickens, four doves, four turkeys and the ex-Prefect of the town of Salgueiro perished as a result of stings from wild bees, lately arrived from the South. In the same paper, a short article by the local State Secretary for Agriculture recounts that orópa bees, enraged at not finding suitable accommodation for their queen, had slain a horse in the State of Alagoas. Perhaps the bees in the caatinga, seeing how poorly the human beings were housed, were less inclined to be demanding.

Some way further along the trail we came on another hut. This was made of packing cases marked 'Food for Peace' and roofed with anything which could be held down against the wind, making the wattle-and-daub walls and tiled roofs seem lordly in comparison.

Propped against the hut was a thin figure, its head covered with a cloth – perhaps an old woman of forty-five who had survived the hazards of childbirth to become a grandmother at twenty-eight or thirty.

We regained the jeep and set off along a track made by the Padre's men to see the land for the experimental plantations. A small part had already been cleared and fenced.

'All this land will have to be cleared eventually,' said Alcibiades, 'and it will take many months. Of course with a tractor we could do the job much more quickly, but they wouldn't know how to look after it . . .'

'And you wouldn't know how to pay for it,' muttered Padre Lorenz.

'What about sisal?' asked Kenneth. 'I was talking to an expert in Rio and he said that the price had dropped sharply and he didn't consider it a good bet.'

'With our low overheads the price would be satisfactory,' said Alcibiades and the Monsenhor supported him later, instancing a cousin in Remanso who had done well out of his plantation.

'And what about the labour?' enquired Kenneth.

'That is the trouble just at present. The older men don't understand the concept of organised agriculture and we shall have to begin with the young ones who have been through school, hoping that the others will follow. Over there,' he pointed into the mato, 'three or four small lakes form after the rains. If that water could be conserved, our problem would be much simpler.'

There was a whoop and a cloud of dust and Pericles came pounding towards us, leather hat over one eye.

'Does he live near here?' we asked.

No, he's just interested,' replied Alcibiades.

18

No special plans had been made for Saturday, but the Padre told us at breakfast that there was to be a wedding at ten. 'I almost forgot.' His pock-marked face crinkled.

'Oh, you mustn't miss that,' said Monsenhor Nestor. 'You, Dona Peggie, can go with the women and dress the bride. She will stand quite stiff like a doll with her arms outstretched while they strip her and dress her again.'

Shortly before ten, the bride and groom rode up, and their horses were tethered to a tree. Padre Lorenz opened the door of the small guest room where he had been sleeping. This was to be the dressing room.

The saddle-bags had hardly been lifted from the horses when another couple rode up.

'*Quema*,' whispered Dona Nilsa. The second bride, a handsome sulky-looking girl with muscular forearms, had run away from home with her bold-looking bridegroom and would have to face an irate father on her return. She was twenty-four, old for a bride in these parts, so perhaps the father's opposition had been long-lasting, or maybe she had compromised herself to avoid spinsterhood.

The saddle-bags were brought into the small room and the door carefully closed. The first bride, young and rather shy, unpacked a cotton wedding dress, starched but rather crumpled. It was touchingly trimmed with frills and small bows of the same coarse material. Her outfit was complete with white cotton stockings and shoes, and fresh underclothes, the bra frayed with much washing. She had a white tulle veil and a little purse to dangle from her wrist, and had evidently taken great pains to contrive her wedding apparel.

The runaway bride, since the whole operation was clandestine, dared not make a wedding dress but had brought a short cotton frock, part white and part striped with pale blue. But the Padre, always resourceful, had a box full of dressing-up clothes for an occasion such as this, and out of it came a tulle veil fixed to a white beaded band.

Turned modestly to the wall, the brides one after another were stripped and dressed. Conceição sat the first bride on a chair and combed her hair, bunching the long strip of tulle prettily on her head.

Just then, there was a stir at the door and a third bride appeared. Sullen-looking, with scrubbed wooden features and the wary expression of a neglected animal, she stood uncertainly in the doorway.

'She's going to marry a widower, the father of two of the pupils,' explained Dona Nilsa, 'those two pretty girls who showed you the parakeets flying in the trees. They have never seen their stepmother before. She lives on the other side of Curral Novo.'

The two daughters, who would not have looked out of place in any gathering in Rio, shook hands gravely with the woman and one wondered what sort of a relationship would grow up.

When all three brides were ready we went to meet the bridegrooms who had, meanwhile, been to confession for the first time in their lives, and everyone trooped into the chapel. We were invited to stand beside the altar, having refused the chairs which they offered.

The runaway bridegroom made his responses with a noticeable lack of enthusiasm.

'Show a bit more ardour, man,' said the Padre and went on with the service.

Afterwards, all three brides, still in their wedding finery, mounted their horses to be photographed by Padre Lorenz.

'It's not right,' said Padre Lira frowning. 'No woman would mount her horse until she'd changed her dress.' But Padre Lorenz, quite undismayed, continued to take his pictures, and the brides seemed happy enough.

That evening, our last in the caatinga, as we rocked slowly under the stars, Monsenhor Nestor told us of the strange customs of the country – of the *lobisomem*, the werewolf of the sertão, and the *rezas* with their spells. He described the customs of the 'afilhados'. These are a pair of people, young or old and of either sex, though never two adult men, who dedicate themselves to a lifelong friendship. On the Eve of St John they dance round the fire singing 'São João was sleeping, São João awoke, this is my afilhado whom São João bestowed.'

'When children's milk teeth fall out they throw them on to the roof and cry, "Ramão, Ramão, take back your bad tooth and give me a good".'

'Who is Ramão?'

'Nobody knows.' The Monsenhor turned to Alcibiades. 'You remember the old saying, "Couro curtido nem Deus dilacera" [leather which has been tanned not even God can tear] that is a corruption of "Cor contritum Deus non despicies" [a contrite heart, oh God, wilt thou not despise].'

'There seem to be very few people with saints' names here,' I remarked, 'not at all like the Spanish-speaking countries.'

'Brazilian parents really enjoy expressing their originality,' replied Monsenhor Nestor, 'perhaps because their families have always been so large. You probably noticed the popularity of classical heroes' names like Pericles, Cicero and even Venus, a little black boy I knew . . .'

'And Alcibiades and Nestor,' I added. They both smiled.

'And then there are all the names which seem to have come from your country – Wellington, Nelson, Newton and Edison and so on,' said Alcibiades.

Monsenhor Nestor intervened. 'And what about the wishful-thinking names like the senator's wife who hopefully called her ninth child Ultimo and then had three more?'

'And that clerk in the Ministry of the Interior who heard the word "éclair" and asked what it meant. When they told him it was something sweet, he named his eldest son "Eclayr" and the next two daughters "Ecledyr" and "Eclenyr".' (This habit of adding a suffix to vary a name appears to be of Indian origin and is very common in Brazil.)

'The best of all,' said the Monsenhor, 'are the home-made ones using half the name of each parent, like Waldyra (Walter and Jandyra) or Nilsa (Nilo and Elsa).'

I thought of all the bungalows in our country named according to the same system, and how much more attractive it sounded in Portuguese.

'The wife of one of our Ambassadors has the prettiest name, "Céu Azul" or blue sky. Too bad I only heard it after my last daughter was born,' twinkled Alcibiades.

After supper, the room gradually filled with people. Dona Ana and Raimunda, the cook, Miguel and the 'gipsy' mother with her brood, and everyone belonging to the Fundação, squeezing into the narrow space behind the dining chairs.

There was a hush, and then the Padre rose and made a little speech, thanking everyone who had worked so hard to make the Concentração a success.

'Seu Kenneth, will you say a few words? We would like a record of this day . . .' The tape recorder stood on the table before him.

With great aplomb Kenneth made a little speech and the microphone was pushed towards me. But my voice soon failed me. These people were so utterly lovable and we would, perhaps, never see them again.

The Monsenhor's sermon was played over, there were abraços all round, and before nine o'clock everyone was in bed in preparation for the 5 a.m. start next morning.

It was dark when we left the Fundação in the jeep with Alcibiades, the Monsenhor and Senhor Pedro's eldest daughter who, like the professoras following in the Rural with Padre

Lorenz, were being taken to see us off. We were to stop on the way at Aramarí to eat our merenda in the old Colonel's house.

For a time we could see the dust cloud raised by the Rural and then it disappeared. We reached Aramarí about eight-thirty. No one was on the verandah, but as we knocked the whole family came out to welcome us.

'We expected you yesterday,' the old man said. 'We waited all day.'

Colonel Mariano's beautiful old wife took me through the house and into the garden. For all the old man's modesty this was a rich man's house in terms of the sertão. On a wooden ledge outside the kitchen stood rows of hand-made clay bowls full of milk and cheese. Pots like Roman amphorae were held in the crooks of great branches thrust into the ground beneath the eaves.

The Senhora took a handful of corn and called, and in a moment she was knee-deep in bloomered hens with glossy speckled plumage.

'Those are a *carijó* breed,' said Monsenhor Nestor. 'Has the Senhora perhaps a few fertile eggs?'

The old lady returned with a clay pot containing three smooth white eggs which she handed to the Monsenhor.

'Would the Senhora like some corn?' she asked me.

As I threw it on the ground turkeys came gobbling up with a number of small, darting bantams.

'The male turkeys are quarrelsome,' said the Senhora. 'They will fight over a hen, but they won't hurt you.' A turkey, his dangling dewlap inflamed almost to bleeding point, had made a sudden lunge.

'Come into the orchard. That is a sour sop,' she pointed to a tree bearing pale green fruit with crocodile-skin markings. Amongst the pomegranates, bananas, persimmons and papaws were tamarinds with feathery leaves and fragrant yellow flowers. The fruit can be eaten with salt, or makes a refreshing drink if it is soaked in water for two or three days while it is still green.

A pupil, with the badge of the Fundação on her pale blue shirt

Children arriving at the Fundação school. Most of them have to walk – sometimes as much as eight miles

Homework. A younger brother looks on enviously

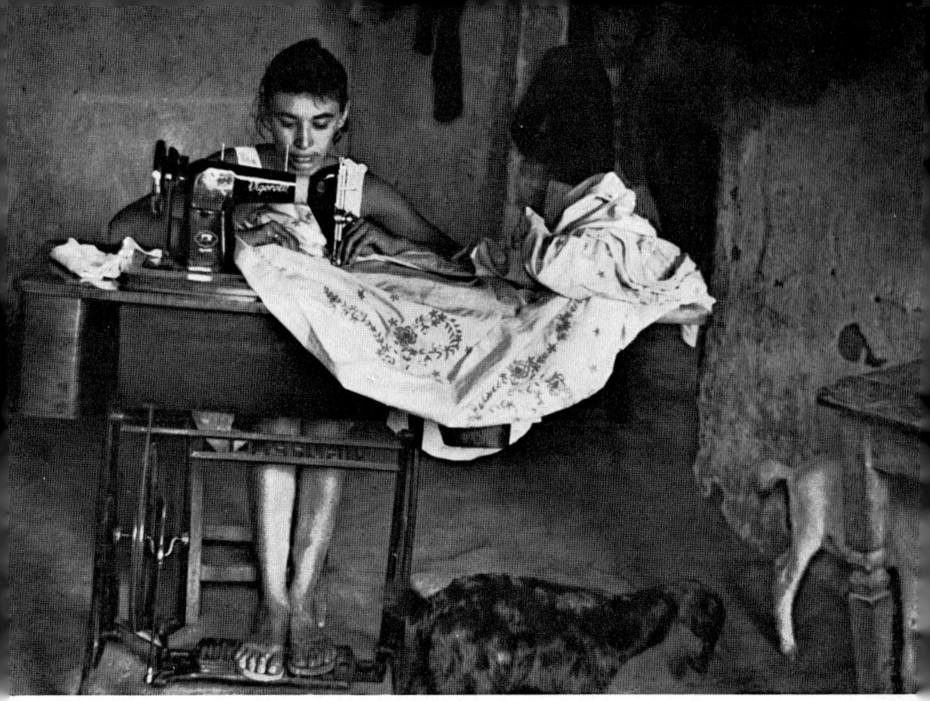

Industrial revolution in the caatinga. A girl works on a delicate piece of embroidery while the goats frisk round the earth floor of her home

Conceição with samples of embroidery

Children leaving their improvised schoolroom, the chapel at Cacimbas

We sit beside the altar as Monsenhor Nestor celebrates mass at Curral Novo; the home-made Union Jack in the background

'May I see your garden, Senhora?' I asked.

She took us to the walled enclosure at the side of the house and showed me bushes of tiny scarlet *malagueta* peppers which are so fiery that a couple of drops of the vinegar in which they have been steeped will season a whole plateful of food.

A plant with bronze leaves bordered in white and small scarlet flowers was hanging in a basket.

'This is called "showers of money", and there is a "friar's pate".' She pointed to a globular cactus crowned with a skull cap of scarlet petals.

A tall vine was covered with elongated gourds. She slit one open to show a loofah stuffed with black seeds.

'We use them for cleaning our pots. I will give you one.'

This loofah was used in our shower in Rio for many months and we frequently slipped on the black seeds which continued to emerge.

'That is a shoe-shine plant.' To my surprise she picked a double hibiscus flower. 'If the Senhor will hold out his foot . . .' She bent and polished Kenneth's shoe, which took a beautiful shine.

Aramarí was an oasis filled with good things. I wondered how it would look when the sun had scorched up the sheet of blue water in the hollow below, and how the plants would survive the blazing days.

The men had gone into a large open shed behind the house. Curls of orange peel were drying in the rafters.

'Look,' said the Monsenhor, 'this is the machinery for making manioc flour which I was telling you about. The manioc is lifted by hand and brought in by the men, then the women scrape the roots and soak them in water, squeezing out the poisonous juice. This has to be thrown away quickly or the animals drink it and die. For some reason, they like it very much.'

'You can accustom an animal with patience, giving it a little more each day,' said the Senhora. Like Nero gaining immunity from poison, I thought. 'And then they grow fat.'

'The manioc is put through a crusher,' resumed the Monsenhor. He showed us a toothed iron cylinder operated by a thick cord running round the groove in a wooden wheel.

'This is turned by two men, pushing with all their strength. The machine is lubricated with suet. First a white liquid comes out and is poured into wooden troughs. As the water evaporates, the fine white "tapioca" is deposited.' A bowl holding a layer of powder stood on a bench outside.

'Take some on your finger,' said Monsenhor Nestor. The powder was as fine as starch and had an indefinable pleasant taste, quite different from the gluey pudding of our childhood.

'The rest of the pulp is put into an oven and dried to make the type of bread which we ate at the Fundação every morning. The fire is very hot and the manioc is kept moving with rakes.'

'Every bit of the manioc is useful,' said the Senhora. 'The leaves make fodder and the stems are used for fattening the pigs.'

'And you can make *tiquira* from manioc. A couple of glasses of that and you're tipsy,' he added. 'The preparation of the manioc lasts sometimes for two or three months. I remember it when I was a child. It was a jolly time with bonfires at night, and sometimes we danced to an accordion. Friends used to come to help and stay, maybe, for a month. When the pulp is squeezed by hand, the guests are allowed to keep the tapioca.'

'They have some new machinery for making manioc flour,' observed Alcibiades. 'Padre Lira saw it in São Paulo. One mill can turn out a hundred sacks in one day, where it takes six people slaving from sunrise to sunset to make four sacks here. Even simple machinery to make eighty sackfuls a day would cost eighty thousand cruzeiros, though,' he said sadly.

Over large areas of Brazil, manioc is the staple diet which the Portuguese settlers adopted from the Indians. In the eighteenth century the Kings of Portugal ordered that the fertile black soil of the coast of Pernambuco should not be wasted on growing mere everyday food and the Brazilian sociologist Gilberto Freyre remarks on the miserable diet of even the rich landowners of the North-East who, until recently, neglected the cultivation of vegetables and all but the most ordinary fruit. Even the Cariocas of Rio, not so many years ago, were little interested in vegetables and it was the Japanese immigrants, with their wonderful nursery gardens, who finally introduced abundant green vegetables and salads to the markets.

Some time had passed and the Rural had not yet arrived.

'Better not wait,' said Alcibiades, and the Senhora led us into the parlour, where we sat round a table and ate the flat bread and goat's cheese and chicken we had brought with us, and were offered sticky blocks of sweetmeat made with home-grown fruit, all sullied in my mind by the clustering flies in the kitchen.

On Alcibiades' request the Senhora opened the 'oratorio', a wooden cupboard containing a miniature altar. This was a little disappointing as certain of the older carvings had been replaced by plaster objects. On a side table stood some pretty ornaments. The Senhora explained that these were made by her elder daughters – themselves grandmothers – by patiently cutting diamonds of cardboard and covering them with scraps of cotton and tinsel. These were sewn together to make three-dimensional stars.

Colonel Mariano pointed proudly to the floor, unique in the whole area. Wooden blocks were laid in the form of parquet straight on to the beaten earth. In the dry air of the sertão, wood remains as firm as stone.

A series of whoops outside told us that Padre Lorenz had arrived with his professoras.

'The girls got seasick,' he beamed. 'They aren't accustomed to such a rough ride.'

However, they all sat down happily and made up for a lost breakfast.

Soon we were on our way again and at last the spires of the twin cathedrals of Petrolina and Juazeiro came into view. We asked the whole party to lunch with us in the Saldanho

Marinho and all twelve of us were grouped at small tables laid out like a game of dominoes to fit into the shade of the tattered awning. Melita, at Kenneth's invitation, sat down between us. Padre Lorenz had his arm kindly round the prim little professora Diva.

'I want her to have a happy day,' he whispered to me in German, 'she has so little fun.'

Plates of steak and fried potatoes together with river fish, ecstatically chosen by the professoras, were hurried up from the galley. Out of bottles stored in a fridge with a clanking motor a stream of iced beer flowed down our dusty throats.

Melita looked uneasy. I wondered if she felt the effects of the journey. Suddenly, she stood up.

'Will the Senhor change places with me?' she said. 'The Senhor should be next to Dona Peggie.'

Protocol once observed, she beamed with handsome enjoyment for the rest of the meal.

'So you're flying back to Rio?' asked the proprietor.

'Yes. We have to be at the airport at two-thirty.'

'Two-thirty? Why, your plane leaves at two! I was at the airport myself this morning.'

Now our tickets were clearly marked 'Arrive at airport at 14.30,' but this was Brazil. So now we must hurry, and as we reached the outskirts of Petrolina the plane circled in to land. With country casualness we were allowed to group for our photographs on the mobile steps while the passengers waited patiently for release.

A few moments later we were waving goodbye to the small group, and flying once more over the road leading in a straight line to the Coast and the great world of false values.

19

A MONTH after we returned to Rio, Muriel arrived. Fortunately, August is winter in the Southern Hemisphere and the climate was quite pleasant. (Strangely enough, 'winter' in the caatinga corresponds with the rainy season, which takes place during our English winter. This can be confusing.)

A few days later Padre Lira arrived in Rio and he and Muriel met for the first time. For both, it was a complete fulfilment, a quiet affirmation of the trust and affection which bound them so closely.

From his heavy bag the Padre produced an eighteenth-century crucifix and a small baroque Virgin of the Conception which had belonged to his family, both carved in wood, their colours dim from the passage of time. He handed them to Muriel. 'For my mother,' he said.

We left them to talk, she in Spanish and he in Portuguese, and afterwards, on the terrace of our flat, took photographs of them side by side against the background of the Sugar Loaf across the bay. There were other meetings and finally a rather touching farewell, though no sense of parting.

When the Padre had left, all three of us set to work to plan what could be done to help him. Appeals to various local organisations were not successful, but Muriel obtained an audience with the Papal Nuncio who received her kindly and assured her of his interest. Nothing concrete resulted from this.

A report on the Fundação was sent to Dona Yolanda, wife of the then President of Brazil, who replied that both she and her husband had been quite unaware of the conditions in the Padre's area and promised support. The matter ended there, but at least her letter brought temporary comfort.

Back in England, Muriel, helped by her friends including the girls at the school where she taught, resumed her tireless fund-raising efforts interspersed with letters of appeal to charitable organisations in various countries. Her correspondence with Padre Lira was resumed, now with an added depth through personal contact.

In September the Padre wrote to us with an encouraging piece of news. 'As you know, your visit to the Fundação was reported on Radio Teresina. Now, quite unexpectedly, we have received from the education authorities furniture for the wretched school at Curral Novo. This, at least, is a step forward.'

The Padre had succeeded in obtaining a loan from the Bank of Brazil in Remanso for the construction of the shoe factory. During the long hot days of autumn the foundations were dug and the mud-brick walls rose from the ground with surprising speed.

'*Ritmo de Brasilia*,' said the Padre. Every Brazilian knows of the almost magical rate at which the city of Brasilia was conjured out of the empty sertão by men working in shifts all round the clock. The building, like all the others at the Fundação, was low and well-proportioned. Beside it stood a cabin for the generator, which included a dark-room for future photography.

By the end of October the work was finished. The heat was unbearable under the forced draught of a hot wind – sure sign that the rains were still far off.

The Padre was goaded by a devouring impatience. If only they had the generator and the promised technician, work could start and there would be shoes for sale in March when the school year began in the rest of the State. As it was, the machinery was now all in position, but without electric current only served as a source of wonder to the catingueiros.

On November 11th the manager of the Bank of Brazil in Remanso came with three of his officials to 'receive' the new factory building. The Padre had gathered people from round about and arranged a little ceremony. The manager rose to the occasion and made a speech. Never in his four years in Remanso, he said, had he seen a loan better employed. The whole region, he went on, owed a debt of gratitude to the people of England for the aid which they had sent – the machinery for the factory, the reservoirs and the jeep.

'You cannot imagine how much our work is identified with England in the minds of the people here,' wrote the Padre. 'I wish you could see the factory building. It is well built and solid – worthy of any capital city. Now all we need is the generator and a technician to teach the apprentices, and then we can get to work.'

We discussed the shoe factory with an engineer friend in Rio, who told us that with the help of the Governor of Piauí he might be able to obtain a free generator by January. A year before, we should have been elated, but we were beginning to understand that in Brazil official promises are sometimes no more than an expression of goodwill, and that the Governor's help was problematical.

At term's end there were special celebrations at the Fundação when fourteen of the pupils completed their full three-year course of primary education.

'It was a triumph,' wrote the Padre. 'All of them came to us illiterate and unskilled and now each of these girls has a sewing-machine and a secure means of earning her living, while the boys look forward to working in the shoe factory. It was a wonderful day with everyone, professoras, parents and pupils, in tears. I was able to keep calm as I had guessed what was coming and taken a sedative.

'Of the eight girls who left, one is to teach embroidery in Curral Novo and one in Fechadão near São Raimundo; another is to take a dressmaking course in Remanso so that she can return here to teach. Two will run the school at Barra do Bonito, and two are getting married. Only one, who lives some way off, is being sent by her father to take a course of secondary education and will not be collaborating with us. Next year I hope to open three more schools and two more embroidery classes, if God will help us to find the money.

'I can now speak with experience of the immense benefit which primary education brings to under-developed regions. In Brazil people often comment on the fact that international aid programmes tend to give preference to university graduates, whereas primary education costs so much less and is so infinitely important for those who have nothing.

'Above all, I am interested in the school building programme for next year. I want to establish a school wherever a road can reach and I hope that perhaps generous friends or organisations will adopt them.

'I have just distributed the last four bales of clothing. We have sufficient beds for normal use at the Fundação but lack bedding, so I kept ten of the blankets. At the beginning of the school year the children will be ragged. If only I could get more clothes.'

Time for us was running short as we had completed our term of service in Brazil and were due to return to England at the end of January 1968.

In Rio, we had been making enquiries about the various ways of building reservoirs cheaply. Australian friends told us that one should line the excavation with heavy-duty plastic, welded on the spot to make a continuous sheet which would be drawn up over the edge of the reservoir and held in place by a bank of earth.

However, Engineer Farias was unfamiliar with this technique and not inclined to embark on the unknown. He pointed out that the ground was very stony and likely to damage the plastic, whilst the sharp hooves of any goat which strayed into the enclosure during building might prove fatal. In any case, he did not know of any source of heavy-duty plastic nor anyone capable of welding it. There appeared to be no point in pursuing the matter further, for the time at least.

A member of a British study group bound for Mato Grosso suggested growing Victoria Regia lilies so that their giant leaves would cover the surface of the water and impede evaporation. Another expert, however, pointed out that the water loss through transpiration would not be much less than that due to normal evaporation, and that the plants would foul the water. In the case of a prolonged drought one would be left with an unpleasant vegetable porridge which would have to be cleared away before rain fell once more.

Another suggestion was a little raft, arranged to discharge droplets of oil on the surface of the water and form a film to prevent evaporation. For various reasons, this did not appear satisfactory either.

During this rather frustrating period, the welcome news had arrived from England that Oxfam and Cafod, between them, had made a grant of £2,200 for the building of reservoirs at the Fundação, Cacimbas and Curral Novo. In order that work could begin at once, Father Leising of CRS, Rio, now a staunch ally, had offered to advance this money.

Work was in progress when, during the first three days of November, nearly two inches of rain fell, bringing construction to a standstill.

'The water is a delight,' wrote the Padre, 'even though it has held up the work. When we have to cook with salt water meals are unpleasant, the beans never really soften and the coffee tastes terrible. Now there will be fresh greenstuff in the mato for the animals.

'November 13th is the day of Santa Luzia. The people of the caatinga believe that if rain falls on this day the winter will be good – that is to say, wet. But even if rain does fall, a heat wave sometimes comes in January and scorches the tender crops.

'Providence has inspired the Prefect of São Raimundo to sink a well at Curral Novo. The water is brackish, but infinitely better than the brine we have had to use, although the visiting engineers suffered terribly even from drinking the new water.

'We shall continue to dig the extension of the reservoir. I have arranged for a wall to be built between the two halves in order to contain the water which remains in the completed digging. If the rain holds off, we should be able to finish the new excavation by the end of the month and line it with concrete in a week or so.'

CRS, Recife, meanwhile, had sent a small group of technicians under the leadership of Engineer Farias to investigate progress at the Fundação. One of them, who specialised in co-operatives, caused trouble by telling the people of Curral Novo and Cacimbas that they should give their labour free.

'We have a saying,' wrote the Padre, 'that an aching belly brings a sore head. The poor fellow must have been hungry as he would not eat goat's meat (which, as you know, is delicious), nor mutton, nor chicken, nor game, but wanted beef all the time and that is the one thing we have not got. What with the brackish water and the heat, he was thoroughly miserable and spent all day in his room listening to our gramophone – when he was not stirring up trouble.'

We had met this man at a conference between representatives of CRS and Oxfam in Recife. He insisted that the Fundação was not 'a true co-operative', in spite of the fact that we repeatedly explained that Padre Lira could not attempt to establish the co-operative system until the people had become accustomed to communal effort.

'I do, however, agree with this young man's opinion that our people are not giving as much as they receive,' the Padre continued, 'but how can one expect the older people who are hungry and ragged and have lived abandoned by their fellows to give without first having received something? The Fundação has only been established for three years but already the young people are eager to give their labour in order to build houses for the apprentices in the shoe factory, knowing that they themselves will only occupy them for a short time.

'The agronomist from CRS took ten samples and said that never in his life had he seen such poor soil. Even sisal would not really flourish and, in any case, with the introduction of cheap synthetic fibres, the bottom has fallen out of the sisal market.

'He was surprised when I told him that we had planted cashews, and that they were doing well and looked as though next year they would bear fruit. These are not like the fronded cashews of the Coast, but have bark and leaves designed to minimise transpiration, and roots which thrust out in a wide radius in order to absorb any moisture which can be found. These trees are extremely resistant to arid conditions and can produce quite a good crop of fruit, like brightly-coloured apples, right in the middle of the dry season. A single nut grows attached to each fruit and the juice, which smells of prussic acid, burns the fingers of the women who shell them. That is why they are so expensive – the nuts I mean – because the output is so small. I am sure that in the developed regions cashews would be shelled by machine and the juice would present no problem.

'The agronomist says we must concentrate on raising livestock, especially goats and hardy sheep. When breeding is properly organised the animals can be sold to pay for food when the crops fail.'

The reservoir of the Fundação was now completely excavated, though unfortunately it was still unlined, since the cement had not been delivered in time. Alcibiades, always inclined to be pessimistic, maintained that the ground was porous and would allow the bulk of the water to seep away.

Cacimbas, on the other hand, was a marvel. A second rock basin had been discovered, leading from the first, so that there was no need to enlarge the original reservoir with dynamite and the natural beauty of the site could be preserved. By leaving a small gap in the bottom of the dam, work could go on even after the rainfall, and once this gap was closed, every drop of water which fell would be held in the solid rock.

We had persuaded Ceris, the Catholic co-ordinating agency in Rio, to sponsor an application to Misereor, the West German Catholic organisation, for the cost of constructing two catchment cisterns for water collected from the roofs of the Fundação during the rainy season.

There are a number of foreign organisations ready to help with projects in under-developed countries. All of them are over-burdened with appeals and their programmes are liable to sudden disruption through the diversion of funds to some major disaster. Each organisation requires an application to be minutely documented and usually accompanied by photographs. One such report may well run into fifty pages, and the Padre had no one to help him with the compilation or even the typing of the final document.

For a man in charge of both the material and spiritual organisation of an area of 8,000 square kilometres, suffering from ill health and obliged to travel in the utmost discomfort many thousands of miles each year, to make even one of these applications is a burden. To make it in the certain knowledge that it may be fruitless is almost intolerable. Nevertheless, working far into the night by the light of an oil lamp. Padre Lira produced, over the years, a series of remarkable reports.

Christmas brought comfort to the Padre.

'Never did I expect such a happy day,' he wrote to Muriel, 'and I want you and your friends to be the first to hear about it. On Christmas Eve I celebrated mass at Salgado, making use of the newly opened road. It is the poorest of all our communities, but very good and faithful. A fine drizzle was falling but in spite of this a crowd assembled. I installed a loudspeaker, with batteries of course, outside the chapel. While I heard confessions, music was transmitted and everybody marvelled.

'Next morning, the rain was still falling and I had to celebrate mass in the chapel, not in the open air as I had hoped. People had ridden in from a great distance and those who could not find room inside were able to follow the service by loudspeaker.

'There are some twenty houses within easy reach of the chapel, and our survey showed that within three kilometres there are about a hundred children under fourteen years of age. They have never had a school and I hope so much to set one up, and pray that God will send us a patron.

'On Christmas Day I celebrated evening mass, first at the Fundação, then at Curral Novo at eight. I was really tired but very happy and now, after a peaceful night, feel quite rested.

'The people of Salgado make hammocks from the fibre of the caroá, which is a plant of the pineapple family. It grows very freely round here and after the leaves are cut and soaked they produce a quantity of long fibres. These are twisted into cords and it takes one man about a fortnight to make a hammock. My uncle Alcibiades gave one to Dona Peggie, who is always interested in our problems, and she has written to say that there should be a good market for them in Rio. This would help the community.

'This year I shall not be able to make my trip to the South as I must be here to supervise the work on the reservoirs and to receive the generator, if it arrives. I much prefer to stay here in the quiet of the caatinga, but we shall lose all the money and materials which I collect on my annual trip to São Paulo.

'Another blow to our finances is the devaluation of the pound, which has fallen from Cr$7.60 to Cr$6.00, and so much of our money comes from England.'

Our engineer friend, disappointed in his hopes of a free generator for the Fundação, had found a secondhand one going for the very reasonable price of Cr$3,500 (about £600 at the then rate of exchange). He promised to send a technician to inspect it and, if satisfactory, to service, re-paint and despatch the generator to Juazeiro on one of his own lorries. We hoped that this problem, at least, would now be solved.

'The delay over the generator fills me with anxiety,' wrote the Padre, 'since we have to repay our bank loan and the longer we delay the greater our debt.

'Medicines too are a problem. Last year we received invaluable supplies from the Catholic Medical Mission Board in New York but this year it has been decided that all applications must go through Caritas and ours has been refused. This seems incredible now that we have at last managed to bring a doctor here once a month. Without medicines, his visits are almost useless. We desperately need vitamins, analgesics, tonics, remedies for liver complaints, dehydration and the treatment of diarrhoea among children.

'After months on the punishing roads the jeep is limping badly and in need of major repairs. Without a jeep and without medicines the doctor's monthly visit will be impossible.'

After Christmas, the rains ceased and the tender crops were scorched by the sudden heat. Half the reservoir at the Fundação was now lined but almost all the water in the other half had been used up in making the cement, so drinking water had to be fetched from Curral Novo.

'At this season a cloud of apprehension hangs over us,' he wrote to Muriel, 'but your words are a great comfort to me and the photograph of us together is one of my precious possessions, something which two years ago I would not have believed possible.'

There was now no hope of a harvest and no news of the promised food from Caritas. If rain should fall, it would be too late to sow again. In bad times, the price of food always rises, and with the steady devaluation of the cruzeiro the price of everything else was rising as well.

To add to the sense of desolation at the Fundação, the

Bishop of São Raimundo resigned his post and the prelacy was left to its own devices.

It was with a heavy heart that we left the Padre with his problems, and the many friends we had made in a country we had grown to love.

PART THREE

A Widening Prospect

20

If in Rio the caatinga seemed far away, in England it hardly seemed to exist at all. Half a dozen atlases showed only a blank for the whole area, with here and there a small town or hamlet picked out for mention in the haphazard manner of maps based on ancient surveys.

A high-powered publicity campaign was blazoning the woes of Biafra. This particular tragedy seemed to enter one's very home and the response of the public was boundlessly generous, but one had an uneasy feeling that aid might not be reaching the people for whom it was intended.

Meanwhile, in the silent caatinga, rain fell at last, at the end of February and again in March, chilling the air and sharpening the prevailing hunger. Few people had seed to sow, and it was now so late that any growing crops would probably be scorched by the increasing heat of the next three months.

Though saddened by the loss of the harvest, the Padre was delighted with the rain. 'All the reservoirs are full to overflowing and the mato is green with fresh wild grazing for the animals. At present we can use water for every purpose – cooking, baths, washing clothes and even the jeep and the truck,' he wrote. 'The vehicles cannot be washed in brackish water as it ruins the paint and encourages rust. It is true that for the moment we are prisoners and cannot move in any direction. I don't even know when the truck will be able to take this letter to Juazeiro, but the benefit of the rain far outweighs any inconvenience.

'I haven't yet reconciled myself to the departure of your brother and his wife from Rio. During the last few days I was unable to work at my desk owing to the rain dripping through the unlined roof, so I passed the time looking at the photographs and slides of their visit. What happy memories!'

It was well over a year after our return before we had finished converting our future home in the country and taming the wild garden, and I was under contract to write another book. So although we kept up a regular correspondence with Padre Lira and followed his doings with the deepest interest, it was not until the autumn of 1970 that I could start active work on his behalf.

'Don't be concerned, Dona Peggie,' the Padre wrote, 'if you are not able to write regularly during this time of stress. I can well understand all that you have to do and the tremendous impact of being in your own country and amongst your family and friends once more. Don't feel that you must write regularly. We can maintain our contact for the time being through Dona Muriel, who gives me all your news. I will send you copies of my letters to her. I feel sure you must rejoice at exchanging diplomatic routine with all its protocol and insincerities for the life of your own home – for a real life.

'An old lady of eighty-one has given me a beautiful silver spur which belonged to her grandmother. Women used to ride side-saddle using only one. The fastening is broken and there is nobody who can mend it properly here, though the repair should not be difficult. I must find someone who can take it to England. The parcel will not be bulky as women's feet were very small a hundred years ago.'

A very large part of the Padre's energy was still absorbed in the effort to raise enough money to keep the Fundação going. Not only was it necessary to lobby officials, but once a promise was obtained it was difficult to see that it was carried out.

'I went to see the Minister of Education in Rio,' he wrote at the end of April 1968. 'When he read my report he said I must be either a saint or a madman. The latter, I am sometimes inclined to think! However, we are opening schools in Salgado and Cansação, making a total of five. An embroidery class is to start in Curral Novo and another in Fechadão, the small parish near São Raimundo where I built a church so many years ago. The people there are very loyal and always ask me to return for the feast of their patron saint.'

When the new school year began in May some of the children were unable to attend as they were in rags. Having nothing else to wear, they had been obliged to use their precious school uniforms when working on the land during the holidays. The Federal Government grant for the schools had not been paid and funds were exhausted.

The Padre decided to appeal to the Governor of Piauí for help. But when he reached Teresina, after a journey of two days over rough roads, the Governor was not available.

All the news was not bad, however. Misereor had agreed to a grant for two catchment cisterns to provide drinking water for the Fundação. These were particularly important during term time. In order that work could start immediately, Father Leising of CRS, Rio, who was now an active supporter of the Fundação, again advanced the money.

'This is the project which was taken to Ceris by Dona Peggie on the very day you went to see the Nuncio,' he wrote to Muriel. 'Afterwards, she persuaded me to return with her for a round-table discussion with the agronomist, Dr José, the co-operative specialist and Engineer Farias. I was reluctant to go as, on a previous occasion they had refused to see me. However, there seems to be something rather dogged about an Englishwoman's approach. They were all helpful and suggested that I should put in an application to Misereor for a grant for goat-breeding as it was the considered opinion of all of them that it is only in this direction that our future husbandry can develop.'

This application was refused, probably since more funds could not be spared for an organisation which had so recently received aid, but the research which went into the application served as a basis for my later request to Christian Aid, which was successful.

At the end of May the Padre wrote that the pressure of supervising road-building, opening schools and running the

Fundação had obliged him even to postpone Mothers' Day celebrations. There was simply not time to visit the various chapels as frequently as before, and the catechism classes were not making the progress they should.

'I await anxiously the arrival of the new bishop,' he wrote to Muriel, 'and hope that he will be understanding and dynamic too and give me an assistant. You suggest a British volunteer, but conditions here during the drought are at present such that no one who is not a native of the region could stand them. Eventually, I hope to train one of our pupils to take over the administrative work but there is no one who is ready yet.

'Mothers' Day, when it was finally held, was delightful in spite of the fact that we had not enough presents for all the children. We chose as Mother of the Year a poor woman with a family of thirteen. The couple sat by the altar surrounded by all their children. I am not in favour of such large families as the burden on the mother is intolerable, but it is important that such women should feel that their sacrifices are recognised.

'The Pope's encyclical on birth control has aroused a good deal of feeling in the big cities of the South. The clergy are divided and the Catholics confused. My own impression is that those who favour birth control will continue to practise it.'

The question of the generator was beginning to cause great anxiety. We had left Rio confident that it would be at the Fundação before we reached England, but there was still no sign of its arrival. Until the generator was installed it was no use bringing from Franca the technician who was to teach the apprentices to make shoes. Interest on the loan from the Bank of Brazil had to be paid and the first instalment was now overdue. Instead of production being well under way, it had not even begun.

On careful examination, the generator first proposed had proved unsuitable. Brazil is a country where machinery tends to be used until it falls apart, and good second-hand equipment is very hard to find. In response to a number of advertisements, an apparently sound generator had at last been located, but this would cost Cr$6,000 instead of the Cr$3,000 set aside for the first machine. The extra £500 could be paid in instalments.

During June, an American came to inspect the roads which had been built with Food for Peace distributed by Caritas Brasileira and seemed rather surprised to find that they really existed. As the jeep belonging to the Fundação had broken down, he had to cover the great distances in a hired vehicle, which proved very expensive for the Fundação. The representative confirmed the disturbing rumour that oil and corn would no longer be supplied by the Americans, since Brazil was exporting both these products. However, he thought it possible that his government might change its mind in the case of the North-East.

'The American was deeply touched by the sight of mothers with small children in their arms begging for scrapings from the school meals,' wrote the Padre, 'and to see some of our children giving a share of their precious food to the little ones.

'I explained that in normal times the diet of the people here includes fat and protein from the milk and cheese of their animals. If the oil is withdrawn, the little food they now receive will be almost entirely farinaceous. One of the mitigations of the drought is that wild creatures become easier to shoot, and men can go out with their guns after a day's work. Rock cavies, armadillos and prairie rats cooked with a little oil are all quite palatable. Without it, they are dry and stringy.

'I have written several times to Caritas to know whether supplies of oil really are going to be stopped, but they simply don't answer my letters. There is nothing for it but to go to Salvador.'

There was still no sign of the promised government grant. 'I am afraid this may be due to the present clash between the authorities and the Church,' wrote the Padre. 'During recent conflicts with the establishment many priests supported the workmen and the students, and all the bishops signed a protest. Nevertheless, I shall go to Brasilia on August 16th and apply for a grant for next year. Unless the application is made and funds voted, one has no hope at all.'

The rest of Brazil was now enjoying school holidays and one of the Padre's many sisters visited the Fundação with her seven children, bringing their hammocks and provisions and a servant to help with the extra work.

Padre Lorenz, who had added so much to the enjoyment of our own visit, also arrived with camera and ciné equipment. After our return to Rio we had grown to know and appreciate this remarkable man. The son of a baker in the small town of Sigmaringen near Lake Constance, he had grown up in the grim years of the First World War.

'My father was determined that I should take over the shop as I was the only boy, and I made wonderful tarts by the time I was five years old,' he told us, 'but my mother, who was a strange solitary character, was sure that I had special talents and resolved that I should have a good education. My father would not do anything to help, so there was nothing for it but the Church. A friend told me there were good openings in Brazil, so as soon as I left the seminary my mother packed me off. We said goodbye at the railway station and I never saw her again.'

Perhaps it was loneliness which made Padre Lorenz take up music with such passion. His mother had certainly been right about his exceptional gifts. During the years he spent as a teacher in Salvador de Bahia he became a musician of a very high calibre. But like a tough old tree, his almost Protestant sense of independence refused to bend under a discipline which he found unjust. Finally, the Father Superior sent him to Coventry for a whole year and also forbade him to conduct any concerts or choirs. During this year of enforced silence and deprivation his resentment gradually became bitter. Eventually, Padre Lorenz was transferred to the Benedictine Monastery in Rio, where he worked once more as a teacher. But even here, there were various practices with which he could not agree and after thirty-five years he went out into the world again.

When amongst simple people, Padre Lorenz was full of an infectious gaiety and the most sensitive kindness. Alone, he was subject to fits of intense melancholy. It was this dark side of his character which impelled him to give up music for ever after leaving the Benedictines. His friends pleaded with him in vain, but no one could dissuade him from this self-mutilation.

A friend found him a chaplaincy at a nominal salary in the ship-building yards in Niteroi on the far side of Rio harbour and some nuns took him in. The toughness which had caused him so much trouble in the past and the creative talents which his mother had divined saved him in the new situation, and he was soon earning a sufficient income by taking photographs which he developed in his bedroom during the hours of darkness. So it happened that his old pupil, Padre Lira, had asked him to come and spend the holidays making a photographic record of the Fundação.

'Padre Lorenz was, at first, too tired to sleep, but soon he was off taking photographs all over the place under the burning sun,' the Padre wrote to us. 'Conceição has come back to us too and spends her time scrambling through the mato with Padre Lorenz in search of pictures. It is just a year since your visit,' the letter continued, 'those were the happiest days we have experienced at the Fundação. We played over the tape recording of your speeches and I must confess that many of us had tears in our eyes.

'I have not felt very well recently, but now I am much better. The worst is when one cannot sleep. With the jeep out of commission I have had to ride great distances and since I have grown soft, I find this very tiring.'

At the end of August, the Padre enjoyed a few days of peace. 'The professoras have gone to São Raimundo for the feast of the patron saint. As it was a week-end I could afford them this simple pleasure. The whole Fundação is drowned in silence. Suddenly one can hear the voices of the tiny creatures in the mato. Even the stars seem bigger and brighter in the stillness.'

In September, the Padre received notice that the £119 had been sent by Cafod to Salvador, instead of Juazeiro, and that once more it would have to be fetched. Banking practice in Latin America is different from that of England. If customers are to receive their money they must work for it. Even the simple operation of cashing a cheque or withdrawing money from one's account can take half an hour and involve applying at one counter, waiting patiently until one's name or number is called, then returning to another, working one's way up the queue, signing various forms and finally, unless there is some snag concerning identification or the rate of exchange, receiving the money but leaving the bank vowing to stick to travellers' cheques and a bureau de change in future. The banks appear to extend this teasing to their relations with each other, so that when an English bank transfers money to the opposite number of its choice and not to the bank named in the client's instructions, the receiving bank refuses to make a transfer and insists that the recipient shall go in person to claim the money, regardless of whether this involves a journey of hundreds of miles and many weary days. Often the sum is completely swallowed up in the expense of obtaining it.

In the case of Padre Lira this frustration occurred again and again. An Englishman would have been driven to fury, but on the occasion of this Cafod payment he merely wrote with gentle irony that the bus journey from Juazeiro to Salvador now only took seven hours each way (on top of a two-day jeep ride to and from the Fundação). When he did reach Salvador he found that owing to a local holiday, the bank was shut. However, the frustration of the whole proceedings was alleviated by the subsequent discovery that instead of £119, a total of £520 had been sent from England. This included money collected by Muriel and her friends and £250 very generously donated by the English Grail Community following lectures we had given.

He wrote to Muriel, 'In spite of many sorrows and difficulties and the daily contact with the wretched condition of my people, since you crossed my path my life has contained a series of joys so profound that I do not know how to be sufficiently thankful. I attended in spirit the Brazilian Evening at the Grail and was deeply touched that people who didn't even know us had cared about our needs. With this money, the school meals are assured until term ends in November, and there is so much else that I can do with it.'

Work on the catchment cisterns was almost completed and they now only needed roofing to keep out the dust and slow down evaporation. Unfortunately, there was no one in the 'parish' with the necessary skill for this work and a gang from São Raimundo had to be employed.

Oxfam Canada had contributed £4,200 with which to build three new reservoirs and Engineer Farias had been asked to select the sites. 'He has chosen three places where we are to establish schools and where the water in the sub-soil – all that the people have to drink for most of the year – is particularly saline,' wrote the Padre. 'One is Salgado, 36 kilometres away; another Cansação, 60 kilometres from the Fundação and the third is Ponta da Serra. As you will remember, this was the last chapel to be linked with us by road, as it is 93 kilometres distant. There was formerly a dam here, but it burst many years ago and washed away the hamlet which lay below.

'I visited all these sites on horseback, with Farias, and we were obliged to ride hard in order to cover the ground in the time, taking in our saddlebags sweet water from the Fundação, a luxury which a year ago would have been impossible at this season.

'Our cashew plantation is flourishing, a patch of brilliant

green in the dun-coloured mato. Small fruits are forming and we should have a splendid harvest. The nuts are the cash crop, but the fruit is good to eat.'

No supplies had come from Caritas Salvador since April, so road work and the resulting distribution of food had to be suspended. 'I am overcome by the silence and indifference of Caritas, the increasing misery here and the unconcern of the Government and State authorities,' Padre Lira wrote. 'It is vital to keep up the spirits of the people and make them feel that someone cares about their plight.

'On the 24th September it was the feast of Nossa Senhora das Mercês, so I decided to use some of the money from England to invite people from round about to a good meal. A multitude appeared and there was dancing until midnight. The director of Caritas Petrolina, who is a good friend of mine, had let me have some powdered milk from his own store, so I gave a kilo to each of the mothers. The festa cost £50, but it was as good as a bottle of medicine for each of the guests.'

After this, there was silence for about a month. The dreaded influenza had struck and the Padre himself, weakened by his digestive troubles and the hernia in his throat, had to be taken to hospital in Juazeiro.

On the advice of the doctor who was fetched from São Raimundo the schools were closed for a week and when they were re-opened more than a third of the children were absent. Malnutrition, said the doctor, had aggravated the disease.

'I am up and about again,' the Padre wrote, 'but I lost a stone over this affair. Thanks to the help from England we were able to pay for the medicines from São Raimundo, which cost nearly £100. And to think that Caritas has stocks of medicines from all over the world! I myself saw the list in August. If only we had food, though, medicines would be less important. Hunger is our gravest disease.'

Word came at last through Petrolina that a load of food was on the way. 'And just now, when we are so much in need of it, our truck has broken down. So here we are with food at last, but food that is out of reach.

'After years of constant use on the rough roads the truck is only kept running by a miracle. As for the jeep, the Nuncio wrote in February promising help with repairs, but I have heard nothing more. We have already spent £75 on small repairs and now we need new tyres once more. The cost of keeping the jeep on the road is becoming quite uneconomic and somehow I must get another one.

'Our stock of clothes ran out long ago. Would it be possible to ask Oxfam whether they could arrange for another shipment of clothes from the United States? The Americans have an arrangement whereby a ton consignment of clothes can be brought in at Recife, whereas you will remember that small shipments from England are almost impossible to get through the Brazilian customs. If money were sent instead, then I could get material direct from the factories in São Paulo at very advantageous prices and the clothes could be made up by pupils who are learning dressmaking at the Fundação.

'The news that a representative of Oxfam is to spend two years in Recife is wonderful. As soon as he arrives I shall pay him a visit and invite him to come to the Fundação. I want to show him the results of all that Oxfam has done for us.'

21

WHEN we parted from Padre Lorenz he warned us never to expect a letter from him, so we were surprised and happy when eleven pages in cramped German script reached us by the hand of a friend.

'My last holidays at the Fundação were so magical,' he wrote, 'that I must share them with you. All day long with Conceição I wandered through the mato without watch, keys, money or any kind of obligations. Never before have I lived so completely in the present. At first I thought that Conceição accompanied me from a sense of duty, but gradually I realised that her pleasure was as great as mine.

'Every morning we watched the dawn in silence, seeing how the clouds each day took different shapes. And in the evening, when we returned, the sun was setting, quite unhurried like ourselves. Sometimes we would sit for an hour, not resting but watching the shadow patterns changing on a rock.

'Happiness does not spring from the things around us, but from our reaction to them. So seldom is there time for tranquillity to tune our receivers so that they can pick up the delicate, tiny harmonies of natural sounds. Our eyes are accustomed to strip all that we see for its message – to gather visual meanings in a sort of hasty shorthand – instead of adjusting the lenses to perceive the infinitesimal contrasts of silver, ivory and ash in a withered leaf.

'The mato this summer was drier than when you were here, disconsolate, almost leafless at a hurried glance. I never thought that this simple girl could see beyond the desolate surface of her surroundings and discern with the clarity of microvision the tiny marvels of the land. She has a good eye for a picture and I shall send her a camera when I return to Rio. I have promised to keep her supplied with film for the rest of my life – not quite so generous as it sounds, for I am close on seventy.'

At the beginning of November 1968, in face of the continuing silence of Caritas Salvador, the Padre's indignation boiled over.

'When I go south I shall make a protest,' he wrote to Muriel. 'I know this may cause a scandal and I don't suppose it will do much good, but at least I shall have got it off my chest. Before taking action, though, I shall consult my friends.

'Although it is holiday time and the Fundação is quite empty, I still have so much to do. Seeing what lengthy letters I write, perhaps you can hardly believe this, but you dear mother are the only person to whom I can write with complete intimacy.

'I was worried to hear about your anaemia. You must not work so hard. What you have done is enough. I feel that I am to blame for your tiredness. Do remember that you are not a young girl any more.

'Last week one and a half inches of rain fell and the soil is ready for planting – but the seed? It is really heart-breaking. It was carefully stored in sealed tins, but much of it has been eaten. People were driven to this by hunger and I have nothing to give them. Now they will be in the hands of speculators who exchange one litre of seed for a 'quarta' at harvest time. A quarta measures sixty-four litres. I had hoped to buy seed which we could distribute when the right moment came, but the money from England – and this was the only famine relief we have received – was not sufficient for all the urgent needs.

'If only I had some food to give the people I would not go south, but as I have nothing, it is better to try to obtain help in São Paulo. It is terrible to leave my people starving and with the hardest time before them. When the rains come the wild animals disappear except for the armadillos, which emerge into the open and are easy to catch. Any beans which they have been able to sow will not be ready for three months. The only alleviation is the fruit of the hog plum which will be ripe in a month's time.

'We have had a bitter disappointment. Our cashew trees were laden with fruit which was swelling and just beginning to colour when flocks of birds came out of the mato and settled on the branches which became literally black with them. Within a short time, every scrap of fruit had vanished. It was like a nightmare. The children rushed to scare the birds, but if two or three flew away, twice as many took their places. Our cashews were the only juicy meal in the whole parched expanse. Later, when the wild fruits ripen, the birds can eat at leisure, but it is clear that there is no hope for our plantation.

'The birds of the sertão, like the animals, owe their survival to the marvellous acuteness of their senses, almost to a sixth sense which leads them great distances to find food. It is their extreme mobility which guarantees survival, and the loss of our cashews is a small price to pay for the beauty and variety of our bird life. Nevertheless, it was a setback.

'Work on the cisterns should have been finished some time ago, but the truck let us down once more. On the way to fetch timber and zinc for the roofing of the cisterns it collapsed in the middle of the road to Petrolina, and remained blistering in the sun for nearly a month as there was no one who could tow it to a garage.

'Cement has doubled in price since the estimate for the cisterns was sent to Misereor, so we decided to use what money was left to extend their volume and do without the tank in the roof, which we had planned to supply taps in the kitchen and bathroom. It is the water which is important, and we are used to hauling it ourselves. To our great joy it has just rained heavily. The cisterns already hold a great quantity of water and the reservoir is two thirds full.

'Before going south I shall pay a brief visit to my relations in Bom Jesus in the Gurgueia Valley where I was born. It is six years since I saw them or my parents' grave. Bom Jesus is not far off – less than 300 hundred kilometres as the crow flies – but to get there one must travel almost 500 kilometres over very rough roads. Whilst with my family I shall rest a little in preparation for my journey to São Paulo, which I always find so much more tiring than staying here.'

When the Padre returned from his visit to Bom Jesus he received the news that the grant which the Government had promised for 1968, but not yet paid, would be cut by half. On hearing this, Muriel wrote to Caritas Internationalis in Rome asking for help in paying the salaries, which now amounted to a total of £200 a month for the fifteen teachers.

Oxfam, meanwhile, had offered to pay for the repairs to the jeep and the truck. A brother-in-law of the Padre's, who lives in Ceará, arranged with his local garage to carry out a thorough overhaul of the truck at a reasonable price. This was fortunate, as on the way back it could pick up the load of Caritas food which had at last reached Petrolina and was being stored there.

'The prospect of this food will cheer people. They have just suffered a bitter blow. A plague of lizards, worse than any within living memory, has devoured any crops which were still growing. They have even stripped bare our little garden at the Fundação.

'A drought seems to throw the wild life of the sertão out of joint and produces plagues of creatures who are normally shy of human beings or nocturnal in their habits. In 1792, there was a famous plague of bats which attacked people in broad daylight, and after the terrible drought of 1877 rattlesnakes swarmed in the caatinga and killed numbers of the survivors, both men and animals, and were themselves killed, hundreds at a time. Infestations of snakes like the deadly fer-de-lance, which normally avoids human beings but becomes bold through hunger, are not uncommon after any long drought, but there is nothing on record to compare with 1877.

'As soon as the truck brings food from Petrolina we shall organise road gangs and the thought of this has given the people fresh hope.

'On January 7th I shall leave for São Paulo by bus. It is a tiring journey, three days and two nights without stopping, but this saves hotel expenses. Aeroplanes have become so expensive and my cousin can no longer get me free tickets.

'This time I must settle the matter of the generator once and for all. The shoe-making machinery is deteriorating and my patience is really running out. Cafod, with great generosity, has sent £800 towards the increased cost of the generator, and I am terribly concerned about what they and Oxfam will think about the delay in getting the factory started.

'One of the most urgent reasons for needing an assistant is to have someone responsible at the Fundação when I am obliged to be away. My colleagues in São Raimundo never visit my "parish" in my absence.

'This is the last letter I shall write to you in 1968, so I send my Christmas greetings to you and everyone. There will be no celebrations this year, but at least we have heard that a new bishop has been chosen and will be consecrated in Rio on March 19th. They say that he is forty-four but looks younger, a Spanish Mercedarian who has been working in Brazil for some years. On April 5th he will take up his office.'

22

THE Padre worked very hard in São Paulo, leaving home early in the morning, tramping the noisy streets, visiting old friends and begging for his Fundação. In spite of the doctor's orders about diet he snatched a quick sandwich in a bar without returning home for a proper meal.

When he did finally go to the doctor for a check-up he was told that the hernia of the oesophagus was quiescent, but that there were signs of varicose veins in his throat. The doctor prescribed an even stricter diet with injections of vitamins and a tonic for the nerves. He had lost three kilos, but after the treatment he felt better.

To Muriel he wrote, 'I don't know how, at your age, you can manage so much work. I am not yet fifty, but I feel so tired and so changed from what I used to be. At night I return home exhausted, without any wish to go out and visit my many friends.

'The people of São Paulo are wonderfully generous. When they hear that England is our greatest benefactor they say that this must be a worthwhile undertaking, otherwise the British would not support it. They begged me to go on television but I refused, because unfortunately I dread publicity. I think that by keeping quiet and praying to God one achieves much more.'

His trip was fruitful and he was able to load the truck, which had been sent down, repaired, from Ceará, with six tons of equipment, including at last the generator.

'But for Oxfam's generous help with the repairs to the truck, the freight on all this would have cost £800,' he reported. 'Even the cost of the petrol and the driver's expenses amounted to nearly £70. Distances in this country are so huge. The return journey took five days, as we had to go via Rio, where Padre Lorenz had collected a lot of things for us. The truck was packed as tightly as a suitcase.

'When we reached Juazeiro we heard that it was raining heavily in the region of Curral Novo and even the jeep couldn't get through. So I decided to make for São Raimundo, where the load could be stored temporarily. But, sixteen kilometres from the town, the road was cut at a place called São Lourenço by a riacho, and the rain continued. It was clear that the truck would not be able to move for several weeks, so we unloaded everything into the house of a friend who moved out of it with his whole family. The generator, which weighs seven hundred kilos, remained in the open covered with a tarpaulin from the truck, as it was too big to go into the house. What a lucky thing that the new Oxfam representative did not try to visit the Fundação as he had planned. He would have had to return to Juazeiro.

'I spent three days in São Raimundo and then decided to risk the journey home by jeep. We took two days to cover the hundred and twenty kilometres. It has not rained so much for years and everyone was delighted. Except for the black bean crop, much of which was washed out, the harvest should be good. The benefit of the rain is so infinitely greater than any damage which it causes. What a glorious contrast with the drought of last year!

'Whilst I was in Rio we had many discussions about my future assistant. Engineer Farias insists that no one from outside the area could put up with the recurrent discomfort, whilst Padre Lorenz, being a German, says that one Brazilian from the south (where as you probably know, there are towns in which until the last war they taught German instead of Portuguese in the schools) is a thousand times better than any padre. Perhaps it would be best to let those two hold a meeting with Father Leising and decide for themselves. All I want is someone who will really work and not just draw his pay.'

A little while later the Padre wrote to Muriel that he had great news. He had been told by Father Leising that Oxfam had authorised payment of the salary of an assistant. By good fortune, the Padre had come upon just the right person, a young man called Benedito Prado, who had completed the second year of his course in a seminary but was keen to work in the field. There had been no time to wait for written confirmation from Oxfam, as Benedito had to come to an immediate decision. Now he was already hard at work. For the first time, with his help, they could have proper Easter celebrations. Many of the necessary liturgical trappings were lacking, but it was in keeping with the new spirit of the Church that worship should be adapted to the means available.

Whilst the Padre was away, a large quantity of oil and powdered milk had been sent by Caritas to Petrolina. Once this had been collected, road work would be starting again. The Prefect of São Raimundo, hearing of this, had offered to take some of the food for his own men and replace it with a sum of money to be used as part-wages for the Padre's workers. This arrangement was useful as it gave the men a chance to buy certain things which they needed.

In May the Padre wrote, 'Benedito is a wonderful asset, full of enthusiasm and ready to take on any job. He visits the outlying communities and helps with catechism classes and social surveys. Work is increasing all the time, thank God. I feel fine, as long as I am careful with my food. Unfortunately, this is not easy on journeys.

'Melita, the professora who organised the quadrilha at the Concentração and accompanied the Bentons to the airport at Petrolina, was married on April 28th and brought fifty of her friends and relations, with all the provisions for the wedding breakfast, to the Fundação for her wedding. Peter Oakley, the Oxfam representative, was here and enjoyed the whole thing very much. He is a delightful young man, very keen on his job and ready to listen to our problems.

'We are now hard at work on the reservoir at Salgado which will be the biggest we have yet made. It will hold several thousand cubic metres of water and be contained by a dam seven metres high. Uncle Alcibiades is supervising the work and Benedito is carrying out a statistical survey to find out how many families will benefit, as well as preparing for the school which we shall open soon.

'The people are delighted at the prospect of fresh water and the men are happy at receiving some of their wages in cash. Fifty of them are working on the reservoir and fifty cutting wood and making the surrounding fence. Formerly there was no money in circulation here and it is something new and wonderful. When our truck fetches lime and cement from Juazeiro, it also brings supplies of simple commodities like coffee, sugar and articles of clothing which the people can buy at cost price plus a small surcharge for the cost of the petrol. Otherwise, they would have to pay the roving traders twice as much. We hope everything will be ready for Peter Oakley's visit on June 17th.

'Yesterday, I was at Cansação supervising the continuation of work in the direction of Ponta da Serra, the lovely road which had to be abandoned two years ago for lack of food with which to pay the men. I left forty men working there. It is the longest road we have ever built and there are still sixty kilometres to go. The community of Cansação is twice as large as that of Salgado and they are eagerly awaiting the reservoir which we shall begin building as soon as Salgado is finished.

'There are now 130 pupils at the Fundação and we could take 200 if there were houses for the families who live far away. Just as last year, the children's clothing is a terrible problem.

The school at Cacimbas couldn't even open as the children are so ragged. As you know, except during the rainy season and at night, when the temperature drops suddenly, no one needs clothing for warmth, so please don't think that I am like those missionaries who hustle the natives into dismal garments and completely upset their way of life. It is the people themselves who want the clothes. They have a strong sense of decorum and do not wish to let themselves or their children be seen in garments which do not cover them in a manner which they consider decent.

'We celebrated Mothers' Day and First Communion once more. Almost all the presents for the children were remnants which I had brought from São Paulo and the new professoras were impressed by the fact that little children of five or six would rather have a remnant with which to make a dress than a doll.

'We are more busy than you can imagine. Every day I make some journey to visit a school or a sick person, then work on a reservoir or the roads, or else go to São Raimundo or Juazeiro. Time is simply not sufficient, but Benedito will soon be able to take over a great deal of this work from me.

'Naturally with so much to do one's health suffers a little and I sleep badly. It is not so much the lack of sleep that I mind, but feeling so ill when I lie down. If only I could sleep sitting up, I think it would be easier. I feel no pain during the day, only when I am prostrate.'

Finally, after a couple of severe attacks, the Padre was obliged to spend a week in hospital in Salvador. There are good doctors there, but he had no friends amongst them as in Rio or São Paulo, so the illness was expensive. The doctor, as doctors often do, advised him to stick to a very bland diet and avoid worry. As a very large part of the Padre's time was spent bumping over the rough roads in the jeep or in country buses, or even on horseback, snatching whatever food was offered, the former advice was hard to follow. 'Dona Peggie will remember the wayside cafés, swarming with flies,' he wrote to Muriel, 'where all you can find to eat may be batter twists fried in oil and some hard sausage.'

As to avoiding worry, the Padre was well aware that the whole existence of the Fundação hung on decisions by various committees hundreds or thousands of miles away, as well as the incalculable administration of food supplies from Caritas, so he could scarcely have an easy mind. Until the Fundação became self-supporting, there was no assurance of continuity for his work. All his hopes were pinned on the shoe factory which, in full production, should serve to supplement the Government grants due to him.

By the middle of April the generator had been installed, but the technician had not yet arrived to teach the boys. However, when the Padre returned from hospital on a scorching afternoon and the jeep was running into the last stretch of road before the Fundação, there was a strange throbbing in the air which grew louder as they approached the wire fence. The shoe factory was working at last, more than a year and a half after the building had been completed and the machinery installed.

The technician was highly skilled and a good teacher. The boys were showing aptitude and the first pairs of shoes, though a little roughly finished, could nevertheless be sold as 'seconds'. The generator was excellent, though more powerful than required for present consumption, and this would mean heavy fuel bills. The only difficulty was the supply of raw materials.

Soon the last scrap of leather was used up. It was useless to expect the technician to remain, idle and far from his family, unless there was a prospect of his having something to do. Application had been made to the Bank of Brazil for a loan with which to buy hides, but in the meantime the wages of the technician must be paid, whether he was working or not, in order to fulfil the terms of his contract. The standstill at the factory was a crushing blow, but an equally severe one was to follow.

On July 20th the Padre received a letter from Peter Oakley

saying that to his deep disappointment the head office of Oxfam had not approved the employment of Benedito. Acting strictly in accordance with the book, they could not sanction payment for any undertaking which was already under way and the news of their agreement had been due to some misunderstanding. The fact that it was almost impossible to find an educated man who was prepared and fitted to work amongst the hardships of the caatinga, and that the Padre had employed Benedito in good faith, believing the project to be approved, did not suffice.

'I have not the courage to tell Benedito,' wrote the Padre. 'He left his job in São Paulo trusting in my assurances and this will be a bitter blow to him. I shall write at once and ask whether Oxfam will not reconsider their decision.'

On this very rare occasion, however, Oxfam put the letter of the law before human considerations.

'I spent the whole of last night without sleeping, listening on the radio to the American landing on the moon,' the Padre wrote. 'Fantastic. I followed every move with the keenest interest. It was wonderful mental hygiene after the disappointment over Benedito.'

The Padre was passing through a period of reverses as harsh and menacing as the drought. But the roots of his faith, like those in the parched caatinga, went very deep, deep enough to sustain life and hope.

It was clearly impossible for one man to continue to run the schools and catechism classes, travel thousands of miles a year to raise funds, deal with the mounting paperwork, as well as supervise all the construction programmes. Now that Benedito's help had been withdrawn, the Padre must find a local substitute who could, at least, cope with some of the simpler aspects of the work.

Four kilometres from the Fundação, at Jacaré, lived a man called Domingos whose daughter, Balbina, had finished her embroidery courses and returned as teacher to the Fundação. Another daughter was teaching embroidery at the newly opened school at Fechadão. From time to time, Balbina was visited by her brother Candido, a young man of twenty-eight who worked in a store at Remanso. Unfortunately, the young man had only a scanty primary education, but he was intelligent and showed great interest in the Padre's work, and he was delighted at the idea of training as an assistant. Unlike Benedito, Candido could not help with the religious and educational activities nor, as yet, with the accounts, but he was young and strong and ready to ride out to the work fronts and lift from the Padre an immense physical burden.

Another problem was finding a suitable driver. There was scarcely a day when the truck and the jeep were not in use. Overworked and elderly as they were, it was not enough to have a man who would flog them over the roads until they dropped. Someone must be in charge of transport who had a sympathetic ear for the first warning noises from a flagging engine – someone who could judge the proper course to take when the truck broke down far from anywhere with a valuable load of food or equipment, shoes or embroidery for sale. Also, he must be scrupulously honest.

Now the former owner of the land on which the Fundação was built was a mulatta named Frutuosas, a little confused in her domestic arrangements, as the Padre kindly put it, since although she had a number of children she had never had a husband. Two of these children had come as pupils to the Fundação and now the boy, José, who was keenly interested in mechanical things, volunteered to train as a driver.

'Like his mother, he is very dark-complexioned, but so different in every other way. I have brought this boy up and he is like a son to me and a very good son. He will have a hard life, out on the roads every day and subject to all sorts of emergencies, but he is happy. And I am too.

'José's sister, Bena, is a very pretty girl,' the Padre wrote, 'but I am afraid she takes after her mother. She has just completed her primary course here and as she is most intelligent I have managed, through Monsenhor Nestor, to secure a scholarship for her at a secondary school in Remanso. She is idle by nature and I hope very much that she will not waste her excellent chances.'

Neither the teachers nor the staff at the Fundação had been paid during the whole year owing to the non-arrival of the government grant. When by the middle of August no money had arrived, the Padre decided to make enquiries. To his chagrin he found that all but twenty per cent of the grants allocated to educational institutions which were not run by the State had been cancelled, though apparently no one had thought of informing the recipients. There seemed no alternative but to close the schools at the end of the month.

However, the teachers, in their enthusiasm, volunteered to work on without pay, though some of them were saving to get married.

Although the material position was so depressing, the Padre was convinced that the Almighty would not let him down. Towards the end of September the novena of Nossa Senhora das Mercês was celebrated at the Fundação. Four days later the news arrived that Caritas Internationalis in Rome, as a result of Muriel's letter, were sending $3,000 towards the payment of arrears on the teachers' salaries.

'Two small comforts have been added to the Fundação,' the Padre told us. 'We now have glass in the windows and this helps very much on chilly nights. Also, thanks to the generator, each room has an electric light, though we do not use this every day, for the sake of economy.

'We now have a small projector which will work for twenty minutes before it heats up. At the end of term I read your letter to the professoras and told them of the help you had sent, and afterwards we showed the slides of your visit two years ago and re-lived those happy days.'

The new embroidery class at Fechadão was turning out even more work than the Fundação. But since with the heavy cost of transport stocks could only be renewed once a year, this meant laying out even more money in advance and a temporary financial embarrassment.

'The jeep, which is taking this letter to Juazeiro,' the Padre continued, 'is going to bring a representative of Caritas to "receive" the road to Ponta da Serra, which is finished at last, in spite of a curious hindrance to the work which occurred in October. The *angico* trees, which at that season appear to be dead, suddenly burst into leaf without a single drop of rain having fallen. Sometimes this is a sign that the rains are near, though not this year, I fancy. The young leaves of the angico contain a terrible poison. Once they are mature, they are harmless. Clearing the road, the men would have had to cut quantities of the fresh foliage and the pack animals, in their emaciated condition, would have seized any chance to devour it. So there was nothing for it but to delay the work for a week or two.

'The Caritas representative was very pleased, and surprised that we had already built 243 kilometres of road. I told him that a detailed report would soon reach the Salvador office. I explained the difficulty of organising road work, which is the only thing which keeps the people going at present, without steady supplies of food. He promised to write to me as soon as he returned to Salvador to say when more food could be expected, but there has been no word from him.'

The apprentices were now making quite good shoes, but it was not worth the expense of transporting these to the towns until the beginning of the normal Brazilian school year in March brought a mass demand. The small stock of leather was again exhausted and so work was at a standstill. The Bank of Brazil agreed to finance the factory in a substantial way, but only once regular production was established. The vicious circle once more!

By the middle of November 1969 there were signs that a drought was building up. No rain had fallen. A week of sudden heat had been succeeded by a return of the cooler weather – a bad sign. The animals were already raw-boned with hunger and even the supply of dry leaves in the mato was running short. The technician, unaccustomed to the privations of the caatinga, sickened and was obliged to return to Franca, and even Alcibiades reluctantly left.

'We listen to the BBC a great deal in the North-East and often hear more news than on our own radio,' wrote the Padre. 'They say that while I was away the BBC forecast a drought this season. Please can you find out if this is true?'

On December 20th rain fell and everyone's spirits rose, to be quickly dashed by the brilliant sunshine which followed. The soil dried out and there was no hope that seed would germinate.

Relations of Padre Lira had offered to pay his expenses if he would come to Brasilia for the wedding of their daughter. The Padre resolved to go, and make use of the opportunity to try and discover the official intentions towards non-State charitable institutions.

'I cannot believe that the Government will be indifferent to the fate of hundreds of organisations which, like our own, are rendering a service to the development of the country,' he wrote.

'The present Government are honest and well-intentioned. It must not be thought that I fail to understand the immense problems with which they are faced. It is impossible to right the ill effects of decades of incompetence and corruption in a few years and they have not, as in England, the support of a nation-wide social conscience.

'On every side there are claims, and some claimants speak with louder voices than others. The under-developed rural areas have hitherto been mute, but now they are beginning to find a voice and the Government is beginning to listen. It is understandable if the authorities, with so many claims on their hands, are tempted to leave those projects which receive any help at all from abroad to look after themselves, but this is a shortsighted policy which will eventually discourage foreign aid. If we should come to grief through the lack of the government grants which are our due, it would be a bad bargain for the State.'

In order to help Padre Lira effectively it was necessary to have a detailed report on his position, but in his overworked state there was no question of asking him to repeat the information and statistics which he had so carefully set out in his 59-page report to USAID. Knowing the excellent technical equipment possessed by American offices it occurred to me to telegraph to USAID headquarters in America, asking if they could kindly send me a copy of the report in question. To my delight, a telegraphic reply arrived immediately from Washington and within ten days the report was on my desk.

23

THE year 1970 began badly. Christmas had been saddened by hunger. Only the animals were able to find a certain amount of food in the natural pasture which sprang from the surface soil of the mato, moistened by the December rainfall.

Since the news media were silent about the plight of Piauí and letters in Brazil so frequently remained unanswered, the Padre decided that he must go to Teresina, Recife and Salvador to find help. This 2,500 mile trip had to be made entirely in local buses, by night as well as day, to save hotel bills.

'My visit to Teresina was very fruitful,' he told us, 'that is to say, if I can believe the promises which were made to me. As a Brazilian, I place quite a different value upon such assurances from that which is placed in England. Nevertheless, I am ashamed to confess – and I hope you will not think me naïve – that I can never escape the bitter disappointment that comes when a promise proves empty. Sometimes I wish people would not raise one's hopes if they do not mean to keep their word, but then I realise that the brief illusory comfort that comes from such hope, even when deep down one recognises it as false, may help to sustain one. So I will tell you about the promises. Take them as you will.

'I went to see the president of the Teresina section of the Leigião Brasileira, a charitable organisation with the wife of the President of Brazil as its patron. The lady in Teresina was delighted when I gave her a large yellow linen table cloth, beautifully embroidered, and told her it was my pupils' work. She assured me that she would visit the Fundação.

'The secretary of the local office of the Ministry of Education promised to pay the salary of a technician for the shoe factory and the Governor of Piauí said that he would send his deputy with a representative of the appropriate ministry to inspect it.

'In Recife I visited an organisation administering a joint USAID – Sudene fund presided over by Dom Helder Camara. The secretary said that this year's funds were exhausted, but that they would have far greater resources in the coming year and would give preference to projects for agriculture and stock breeding. The application, she said, must be fully documented and technically perfect. It is a daunting task, but I must not let this chance slip.' Unfortunately this proved to be one more wasted effort.

'The Director of Caritas for the whole of the North-East was also in Recife and I gave him a copy of my report on the roads which we have built with Caritas food. He was astonished and said that nowhere in Brazil had a programme of such scope been realised in return for their aid. I took advantage of this occasion to explain the difficulties we were experiencing in obtaining supplies, and he told me to let him know the result of my visit to Salvador. When I reached the Salvador office of Caritas, they told me that no food was available for the Fundação. I don't ever recall having lost my self-control to such an extent, and I am afraid that I said a great deal which might have been better left unsaid. Now, once more, I must wait. Patience is not a virtue in Brazil. It is an inescapable necessity.

'In Recife I met Peter Oakley, and could see that he was really upset about the loss of Benedito. Oxfam, he said, was sending £350 to compensate for the expenses we had incurred. Since we had managed to scrape together the six months' salary promised to Benedito, I asked if I could spend the Oxfam money for some other purpose and Peter agreed that it should be used to buy raw material for the factory.

'When I reached Juazeiro on my return, I found £50 waiting at the bank with an advice that £100 more was to follow shortly. This money, which comes from you three and your friends, I shall use to buy seed in the hope that we can still achieve a harvest. Rain often falls in February and March, but we need it at once so that the seed will germinate before the weather becomes too hot.'

Three days later, two inches of rain fell. It was now or never if seed was to be sown but, as always, it was a gamble. The money had sufficed to buy 1,000 kilos of corn and 500 kilos of black beans, in spite of the price rise caused by the drought.

'I divided the seed into six parts,' wrote the Padre, 'so that it could be distributed from six centres, the Fundação, Curral Novo, Cacimbas, Barra do Bonito, Cansação and Salgado. People were told that it came from all of you and this added to their joy. I would have liked to send you photographs of the people receiving the seed, and their happiness, but I found this humiliating for them. I only like photographs which enhance the dignity of human beings, never those which debase them.

'The reservoirs at Cacimbas and Salgado are full to overflowing and the others reasonably well filled. Our own holds enough for half the dry season.

'The famine is still acute, and at best the harvest cannot be ready until May. Even now, the seedlings may be scorched if no more rain falls.

'My friend at Caritas Petrolina has procured for me two tons of food which I will distribute. He really is an ally. I asked for his help when I took the truck to buy seed and he replied, "If England is helping you, can we stand with folded arms?"

'Some of the people are now reduced to eating roots and cactus. This was all too common during the drought of 1950–1. I heard of two families not far from the Fundação who had been poisoned by eating roots which had not been properly prepared and at once sent Candido in the jeep with medicine and emergency food. He managed to save all but two of the children and the rest were terribly ill. But what can I give them instead? The food which has reached us is not enough to go round.'

During periods of famine the people of the dry lands have always had recourse to roots, seeds and strange fruits, with varyingly disastrous results. Many of the things which they eat in their despair are poisonous. Others, suitably treated, would be highly nutritious.

In the past, spasmodic efforts have been made to assess the food value of certain plants which grow freely in the caatinga. Rodolfo Teofilo, who made a close study of the catastrophic drought of 1870, predicted that a plant called *mucunã* was destined to play an important part in sustaining life in the dry lands. He sent a report accompanied by samples of seeds and roots to the Director of the National Museum in Rio, asking for an analysis of their contents. Months passed and then years, and there was no reply. Teofilo said that he was reluctant to ask for help from abroad when his own government was well equipped to carry out the necessary research.

Seven good seasons followed the drought of 1870 and the sufferings of that cruel year were forgotten. In 1888 the rains failed once more, and Teofilo wrote a memorandum accusing the authorities of criminal indifference to the sufferings of their fellow-countrymen.

Eighty years later, Josué de Castro, a nutritition expert and former president of FAO, published in his book *The Geog-*

raphy of Hunger the results of chemical analysis of certain plants of the dry lands which have a definite, though hitherto unassessed, food value.

The most important of these is the climbing mucunã, with it widely spreading tuberous roots. This must not be confused with the hairy mucunã whose stems, leaves and flowers are covered with a reddish down, very irritating to the skin, and whose roots are short and fibrous.

The climbing mucunã produces smooth pods which burst open to reveal four or five large round seeds, either yellow or black, with an extremely hard skin. If the yellow variety are mixed with earth or sand and heated in an earthenware vessel so that the seeds burst open, the pulp can be extracted and pounded to produce a yellowish powder with an insipid flavour and a characteristic bitter smell. This powder must be sieved and then washed 'in nine waters'. Afterwards it is dried in the sun, or in the oven, and forms an edible flour.

Now the people are well aware that manioc, of which they normally eat so much, is very poisonous until it has been thoroughly washed, containing in fact hydrocyanic acid, but they know how to cope with the difficulty and are not afraid of it.

Many of the symptoms of which they accuse the mucunã, the stomach cramps, colitis, dropsical swellings and diarrhoea, are caused by hunger alone, or would have resulted from eating any coarse fibrous food at an advanced state of malnutrition. But mucunã has a bad name which will be very difficult to shake off.

According to de Castro, analysis shows that flour made from the seeds of the mucunã has a protein content higher than that of meat and almost as high as soya, while the calcium content is as great as that of milk. If the pounded seeds are thoroughly and repeatedly washed, the flour will contain no poisonous substances.

Even the roots of the climbing mucunã, properly prepared, yield a greyish flour with a useful protein content. These roots are immensely long and sometimes a yard thick and contain large quantities of water. Early travellers called them 'the fountains of the desert' and were inclined to exaggerate their liquid content, but splitting them with a machete can release as much as half a litre of liquid and there is no doubt that a mucunã growing by the wayside has saved many a flagelado from dying of thirst.

Another plant which grows freely in the caatinga is the *macambira*. This bromeliad, which often forms a dense carpet on the stony soil, grows from a corm containing a quantity of water. During a drought, the animals sometimes tear up the roots and are considerably fortified by eating them. If the corms are boiled and then dried in the sun and pounded, they yield a tasteless flour which, however, is alleged to be fifteen times as rich in calcium as milk and to contain 5% of protein. It is digestible and absolutely non-toxic, but like the mucunã, very laborious to prepare.

The obvious difficulty about using mucunã as a food in time of drought is the lack of water with which to wash it; and people who are starving would find it difficult to produce a worthwhile quantity with the limited strength at their disposal.

Looking from outside, and with no real knowledge of the subject, it appears that in an area where the food position is precarious, it might be advisable, as soon as it is clear that a harvest will fail, to prepare reserve stocks of flour made from mucunã and macambira which could be drawn on when conditions became desperate. Perhaps some simple mechanical device, even the machinery used to prepare manioc, might be used to reduce the labour of preparation.

If people could be induced to try these flours while they were still on a normal diet, it might be possible to convince them that they are harmless. If food supplies turned out better than had been hoped, the flour could be used to feed the pigs and poultry during the period of the year when they usually tend to go short. It would be interesting to hear the opinion of experts on this matter.

On March 19th the Padre wrote to Muriel, 'I am taking advantage of these school holidays to put my files in order and write various reports. The most important is that for the Governor of Piauí. It is vital to give him a clear picture of our needs and achievements.

'As I am quite alone, work is my recreation. I sit down at my desk early in the morning, work until lunch time, have a short rest and continue until six. After a little soup, I work again until eleven o'clock at night. I don't even know how I shall find time to get to the dentist. And talking of this, I had a lovely surprise. The two Filippini nuns through whom you first heard of me suddenly turned up at the Fundação. They had come to Juazeiro, hired a jeep and paid us a visit. I had no idea that they had noticed that some of my teeth were missing and now they write that they have collected the money for dental treatment. How kind they are!

'At the end of February the secretary of the Governor of Piauí turned up at the Fundação unannounced. This was a good thing, as many charitable institutions have fallen into discredit, and by coming unexpectedly, he could convince himself of our bona fides. He was very much impressed with all he saw, especially with the help we had received from England, and said that it was shameful that foreigners should be helping us while the State of Piauí did nothing.

'He left after a few hours, urging me to get my report in as soon as possible. I set to at once and worked until midnight every day for a fortnight. There are twenty-nine close-written pages giving all the relevant facts and figures. "Too long," Dona Peggie will say, but this is the first time that our work is going on record in Teresina and the background must be complete.

'I do understand the very great difficulties with which the Governor of Piauí has been faced. The State is larger than

Great Britain and has only one and a half million inhabitants of whom 80% are illiterate. Until Parnaíba was obtained from the neighbouring State of Ceará in exchange for the town of Crateus, there was not even an outlet to the sea. Parnaíba itself, once a charming place which called itself "the capital of the western North-East", and built a road fifty kilometres long all paved with granite setts, is now a town of unemployed men and empty warehouses.

'The northern part of Piauí once did well exporting the oil of the babaçu palm and wax from the carnauba palm trees, but nobody wants the oil now and the gramophone companies which used to pay high prices for the wax have long since gone over to synthetics.

'The fruit and vegetables grown in the small area of fertile land, and the cattle from the prairies of the north, were largely smuggled over the border into Ceará, where they fetched higher prices, evading the local taxes and bringing no revenue to the State of Piauí. New tax laws aim to deal with this problem and improve the financial position of the State.'

Later, the Padre wrote, 'I took the report to the Governor myself. He said that for this year the State would pay all the teachers' salaries. At the present rate of exchange this represents a sum of about £2,000 a year. He promised a school building for Cacimbas, and another official said that his department would provide two more schools. Peter Oakley, whom I met by chance in Teresina, said he thought that if the promises were fulfilled, it was likely that Oxfam or Cafod would provide the necessary equipment.

'I left Teresina on the 14th and only reached Petrolina two days later, just as the bus was leaving for Rio – another thirty-five hours' continuous journey. After four days' uninterrupted travel I was exhausted and had to rest for two days. God is always very good to me and I came across a friend who gave me an air ticket back to Petrolina.'

The £350 from Oxfam had bought a good store of leather

and once more the factory was working. Some of the apprentices came from long distances away and were unable to get home after the day's work. The Padre had made application to Oxfam for a grant with which to build houses for them, but Peter Oakley wrote that, to his disappointment, this had been refused.

'For the present, the boys can sleep rough under the trees,' wrote the Padre. 'But this is only a makeshift and will certainly be impossible during the rainy season.'

There had been no rain since early March and the precious seed, sown with so much hope, was lost. The drought was building up implacably. Already there were flagelados in the streets of Juazeiro and Petrolina, though no one had left the Padre's 'parish'. The hot wind characteristic of a drought was blowing day and night, scorching the moisture from the earth like a flame gun, drying out the water-holes and devouring what was left in the reservoirs. The larger animals, lacking the cunning of the donkeys, who scratch at the sand with their hooves until they come on a little salt water, or the goats who slake their thirst with the fleshy cactus, were dying. Here and there in the mato their bodies lay like empty sacks until the birds of prey tore them apart and the sharp-toothed ants stripped the skeletons bare.

'The government relief measures for the drought do not help us,' wrote the Padre on April 15th. 'Even if the father of a family goes off and joins a work front he hardly earns enough to keep himself. At present they are paying the men two cruzeiros, or about four shillings a day. The best solution is the road-building which we ourselves organise, when we can get supplies of food.

'The temperature at this season should be quite agreeable, but this year the heat is so intense that one wonders whether freak rains may not fall as in 1932. This would be the climax of misery, as many of the animals manage to exist on the dry leaves beneath the trees. If it rains these turn mouldy. I was only a boy in 1932, but I cannot forget the disaster.'

In May, the Fundação was visited by David Carter, the Oxfam official in charge of Latin American affairs. Through an interpreter, he told the Padre that they would be sending £1,000 for famine relief.

'With the money you and the Bentons have sent,' the Padre wrote to Muriel, 'I am buying seed which will be sealed up in tins to protect it from beetles and other pests and stored ready for use when the rains come. The sight of so many people without seed this year has shown me the necessity of having supplies ready.'

Conceição, having finished her teacher training course, had returned to the Fundação for the new school year and was taking classes all through the morning. In the afternoon she supervised the domestic side of the Fundação, replacing Dona Ana and saving one person's salary.

On June 29th, 1970, the Feast of Saints Peter and Paul, the Padre completed twenty-five years as a priest. Unlike his colleagues, he would have no Jubilee celebrations to mark the occasion, but planned to combine these with Mothers' Day.

'This year we shall not try to give toys to the children, only such clothes and food as we can get. No food has arrived from Caritas, but thanks to Oxfam we can start our road-building again.'

The miserable summer dragged on, the Padre sustained by a faith which went almost beyond reason, and the people by faith in him.

'Thousands of reports on the tragedy of the drought in the North-East lie unread in official archives,' he wrote. 'I myself wrote pages of records, statistics and appeals during the bitter years of the fifties. The lack of communications in those days aggravated the effects of the drought. Our isolation was total. The sight of those endless processions of living skeletons, ragged and drooping, forced to leave their own country where life was simple and innocent, for the degradation which awaited them in the cities, made me decide to dedicate my life to the suffering people of the caatinga. These experiences marked me indelibly, but my emotion then was impersonal.

'Now, they are no longer anonymous victims. They are my friends. These are families whom I know and love. Now, hunger has a name.

'We must endure the drought and our financial torment and keep the Fundação and the factory going somehow. I don't think I have ever needed your prayers so much.'

The terrible news which reached England in June of the Peruvian earthquake and the devastations of the small towns in the Callejon de Huaylas where we had spent such happy holidays seven years before filled us with grief, but also with apprehension that the wave of international generosity would draw with it money which might have gone to the small, unknown projects in other parts of the world.

In September, the Padre received some food from Caritas and road work started again. As the network extended, so the scenes of activity tended to be sited further from the Fundação. In order to provide work for those living near, the Padre decided to build an airstrip. The American Bishop of Juazeiro already ran a Cessna 4-seater and an Interstate Cadet plane, piloted by two of his priests, to the thirty-six airstrips in his diocese, so an airstrip at the Fundação might prove extremely useful in an emergency.

The men entered into the project with enthusiasm. This was progress. This brought the outside world closer. This would put the Fundação on the map.

By the end of October 1970, the airstrip was completed and a small inauguration ceremony arranged. On November 24th, the Cessna appeared – a larger bird scaring the birds of the sertão. It flew low over the Fundação. As it circled the runway and approached to land, school children and road workers and anyone who could reach the spot gathered to cheer. Out of the plane stepped Peter Oakley, tall, sunburnt and dusty, to respond to the Padre's formal speech of welcome and of gratitude to Oxfam.

'It's one heck of a landing strip,' Peter told us later during our meeting in London. 'You know what Padre Lira is. Everything has to be done just so. And the whole thing cost less than £300 and fed goodness knows how many people.'

Owing to some fault, the generator had broken down, and straight away the airstrip showed its worth, as next day the plane returned with a mechanic who put it right.

By the end of the year, besides the airstrip, a further 56 kilometres of road had been added to the total, and the site for a plantation cleared and fenced.

During the autumn, Muriel decided that if her work for the Padre were to be really effective, it must have a firm ecumenical basis. In October 1970, she founded the 'League of Friends of the Lira Foundation'. Its President is an Anglican and the Chairman a Catholic, and amongst its members are those who, from the beginning, have worked and given so generously to help Padre Lira.

In early October we made a journey to Rome and I decided that it was essential to see the person in charge of the Latin American department of Caritas Internationalis and draw his attention to the fact that the Fundação was not receiving from Caritas Brasileira the quota of food allotted to it.

It is not easy to penetrate S. Callisto, the vast papal offices in Trastevere, nor any Italian office for that matter, unless one has a letter of recommendation. I had neither this, nor even the advantage of being a Roman Catholic. However, an acquaintance, herself a publisher and an extremely busy woman, offered to take me down at eight in the morning before beginning her day's work. Trying one entrance after another and climbing innumerable marble stairs, we at last found the right floor and set to work penetrating the first lines of defence.

It was an hour or so before we met with the first clear-cut refusal and I begged Signorina di Luca to go back to her busy office. For myself, I announced that I was perfectly prepared to wait until the evening, hoping that my bluff would not be called.

The interview, which took place about an hour later, was not an easy one, but ended in an acknowledgment by the Monsignore that he was aware that all was not well with the organisation in Brazil and a promise that he would himself write.

Later in the week, the same process of attrition secured me an interview with the director of the Latin American section of Propaganda Fide, which distributes Vatican funds to deserving projects all over the world. A delightful Irishman, Monsignor Conway, listened with interest to my account of Padre Lira's work but told me, regretfully, that funds for the coming year were already allotted.

Viewed from the great power houses of Rome, the Fundação appeared tiny and infinitely distant.

24

THE book for which I had been under contract was now finished and there was time to plan a more active participation in the Padre's problems.

It was clear that the economic future of his area lay in breeding either goats or hardy sheep and, as a native of the region, he knew that the excellent goats of the caatinga were not being fully exploited. For some time he had been planning a pilot project which would teach the younger people, whose minds were receptive to new ideas, how to manage their herds. The local goats were naturally prolific but since they ran wild, a large proportion of the kids were devoured by predators.

If the pregnant goats could be penned, these kids could be protected until they were old enough to look after themselves.

The goats showed a remarkable capacity for survival during all but abnormal droughts, but even in normal years they went through long periods when their condition was too poor either for sale or for local consumption. If the owners could learn to store fodder in silos (and small silos can be obtained for a very reasonable price when bought in bulk), the animals could be kept in condition all through the year. New strains would be introduced to improve the breed, and experiments carried out with hardy straight-haired sheep whose resistance was as great as that of goats, while the cash return was higher.

I prepared a short report describing the condition and needs of the Fundação and went to see the representatives of Christian Aid and Freedom from Hunger. The latter were not able to do anything to help, but Vernon Littlewood of Christian Aid promised, when more funds became available in early spring, that they would contribute to the pilot project.

Meanwhile, news had come through that owing to the exceptional severity of the drought in the North-East, even goats were dying, whilst some of the families, desperate from hunger, had eaten their last animal, thin as it was. The first priority, wrote the Padre, was to see that when the drought broke every family had at least three or four goats with which to build up food supplies once more.

Making out yet another report, I went to see the Administrator of Cafod, which had already done so much to help in building the shoe factory, besides contributing to reservoirs and other things. Noel Charles promised to raise the matter with his committee and later, a grant was made.

On December 5th the Padre wrote to me, 'We are in the middle of the school holidays and normally the Fundação would be deserted but now, the noise of the factory can be heard ten kilometres away, beating like a great heart in the enchanting silence of the sertão. It is the only shoe factory in the whole of Piauí and we owe it to our friends in England.

'I was interested to hear that during your recent journey to Italy you had been to see the director of the Latin American section of Caritas Internationalis and that he had finally agreed that all was not well. You tell me that the director has sent you a copy of his letter to their representative in Salvador enjoining him to reproduce the miracle of the loaves and fishes. This should have an excellent effect, Dona Peggie, though I myself could think of other parables from the Bible which might be more appropriate!

'Our good friend, Peter Oakley, is going back to England for four months leave, but he tells me that he may return to Brazil for another year. Before going, he gave me the wonderful news that Oxfam has authorised a loan of £4,000 repayable in four years, to finance the shoe factory. This is now working in shifts for eleven hours a day. Each day we are making about seventy pairs and I hope that by January we shall be making a hundred.'

'I shall go to Recife to see Peter off,' he told Muriel, 'and buy the things we need for Christmas. The £150 sent by you and your friends I shall use to give the children a little happiness in the midst of the privations they are suffering.

'Peter Oakley is to take some embroideries back for you. Choose whatever you wish and do as you like with the rest. I have given him a pair of shoes, not yet stamped with our trade mark, unfortunately, as this is not ready. I wanted to send a pair to you, but Peter had to keep the weight of his luggage down.

'The longed-for rains have failed to come and only light showers here and there have moistened the earth sufficiently to produce sporadic grazing which draws the animals from the drier spots. Walking so far for food exhausts the unlucky beasts and makes them thinner still, but at least their instinct for finding grazing helps them to survive.

'We have a great quantity of seed stored ready at distribution points,' he continued. 'Each man has a chit so that, when the time comes, he can go to the point nearest his home and collect his share. Like this, when the moment arrives, there will be no confusion or disappointment and no need for people to travel great distances.

'Twelve tons of food – the first of the loaves and fishes – are on the way from Caritas Salvador. Up till now, with the money given by Oxfam for famine relief and the remains of the previous food from Caritas, we have been able to provide for 323 families – a total of 2,290 people – for twenty-five weeks.'

Knowing from his own experience how small hopes and joys can carry one through the grimmest ordeals, the Padre was resolved that this Christmas should bring his children some delight. In Recife he had bought the figures for a crib – something they had never seen before. During the weeks before Christmas the children practised singing and prepared for the ceremony. Portuguese is a strange language, which at a distance sounds a little like Russian. I could imagine the haunting strangeness it would add to familiar carols like 'Silent Night'.

'Our Christmas was the most beautiful in the world,' wrote the Padre afterwards. 'The Christmas of the Drought. No leaves, everything in grisaille. Our Christmas tree was a great dry branch hung with coloured lights and presents. More than three hundred children each received material for clothing, besides sweets, biscuits and a plateful of meat and beans.

'There were so many people that mass was celebrated in the open air, but with electric light everything is possible. The compound was illuminated, a source of wonder to the children. In their small thin faces the eyes were huge and very bright. I was so touched that it was impossible to finish my sermon.

'Next day I left at six for Salgado and here the spectacle was sad indeed. Children who, during the term, had been strong and healthy as a result of their school meals were now small skeletons, pale and listless.

'Nights are still chilly, which means that the rains are far off. Unless God takes pity there will be many deaths. At present, more than a hundred men are working on the roads. Oil was not included in the food which Caritas sent us. There is still £150 left from the famine relief money and I am giving a little to each man for every kilometre worked as long as the money lasts.

'Next week I am going to Teresina to sell shoes and to try and obtain the teachers' salaries promised by the Governor. So far, only five months of this year have been paid. The heat during the day is so great that even I, a native of this country, dread going there.

'This has been a bitter year, with some moments of great happiness.'

25

The year 1971 began badly. Though there were light showers in some parts of the 'parish' no rain had fallen near the Fundação in the three months since November, and the drought was now recognised as a national emergency.

In the more accessible areas men were leaving their homes to flock to the work fronts organised by Sudene. Outside the Padre's 'parish' whole families were struggling on foot towards the towns, some dying by the wayside or suffering from the hallucinations of hunger.

'None of my people have yet died,' wrote the Padre, 'though only God knows how I shall keep them all alive.'

In Petrolina and Juazeiro the authorities, desperate at the number of starving people thronging the streets, were handing out free tickets for lorries to São Paulo in an attempt to avert riots.

The Padre himself made a long and wearying trip to the

south begging for money, food and medicines, and was taken to hospital suffering from exhaustion.

Caritas Salvador sent 27 tons of food to the Fundação. This saved the lives of hundreds of people.

In the mato, the skeletons of beasts mingled with the bone-dry branches of the scrub. All the reservoirs were now empty and on each journey to Petrolina the jeep or truck brought back barrels of water from the São Francisco River.

The leather for the shoe factory had to be damped and afterwards scrubbed with a special soap, but the saline water spoilt its appearance. The technician had beaten a retreat to Franca and the factory came to a standstill.

Isolated by the postal strike in England, we did not know the extent of the growing crisis. Mail taken to Brazil by friends and posted in Rio took five weeks to reach Juazeiro, by which time the strike was over.

During this bitter time the Padre, deprived of the comforting letters from his dear 'English mother', endured alone with his faith.

One night the Padre was working by the light of his oil lamp. Under a brilliant moon the landscape appeared petrified and unreal, the shadows on the ground more substantial than the branches which cast them. This was the white forest which the Tupi Indians had called in their language 'caatinga'. The wandering tribes left it to the birds, the beasts and the snakes. Only the white settlers, disappointed in their search for gold and used to harsh conditions in their native Portugal, decided to carve a living from land which others would never dispute with them. Now, under the moon, the caatinga seemed deserted once more.

'I am quite alone,' wrote the Padre. 'In the great silence one could imagine that the caatinga was empty – empty of all the suffering and of hope as well. Sometimes I ask myself if it would not be better so. The forces of annihilation are so implacable. This is a problem I must face once more as I faced it years ago. Then, it was a shadow battle. Now I have felt the heat and hunger, shared the thirst and disappointment and sorrow, sown the seed and seen it wither.

'Now is the time to draw up a balance sheet, to take stock of the forces for and against us. Years ago, people believed that life in the caatinga was not viable. Even now they repeat this parrot-wise despite the fact that human life has held on here as tenaciously as the seeds which survive ten years in the fissure of a dry rock and spring to life at the first moistening. And it has not held on through any compulsion. Slavery has never existed in this land, nor absentee landlords, nor any great land-owners at all. The people stay because they want to stay, and will return after they have been driven away by drought. They have the same tenacious devotion to their land as the Chinese peasants. If I were to leave tomorrow the people would remain, but their lives would be hard and short.

'The curse of the caatinga is not aridity – man and nature have adapted themselves to that – but the cyclic droughts and the unpredictability of the weather. Our rainy season depends on the movement of distant air masses. In winter warm fronts come in from the sea across the coasts of North-East Brazil. If they reach us, we have rain. If not, our crops are lost and people die. Now, with the marvels of long-range forecasting surely the day will come when we shall know in advance when we can sow our seed and when we must rely on food from outside.

'In the past, drought was a total disaster. Now that we have opened up the country with roads, food can be brought in and distributed and already, our people can give their labour in honourable exchange for the means of survival. Soon, when they have learnt to manage their herds and use their new skills, they will be able to pay for their needs.

'Already, the problem of drinking water at the Fundação, Cacimbas, Curral Novo, Salgado, Cansação and Ladeira has been tackled. Soon we shall have other reservoirs and we shall discover the means to store water on a smaller scale as well.

'Our soil is poor, a thin blanket over the skeleton of living rock, torn away in places by the erosion of flash floods, the exposed rocks in turn fracturing under the burning sun to form wastes of sand. But this same poor soil, after the rains have brought to life the seeds it holds, can nourish a dense carpet of tiny plants which sprout and form seed in a matter of days, giving fresh life to the animals which range it.

'Poverty, ignorance, isolation and neglect have stunted the development of our people in the past, but they are ingenious and have taught themselves to make everything they need in their homes. Like the animals, they use every natural advantage to the full and now that they are at last receiving some care and guidance, they quickly learn to handle even fine materials. This is an untapped vein of human talent.

'The world is suffering from pollution, but we are completely free from it. Even the moral pollution of the cities has not touched us. The code of the catingueiros is old-fashioned and harsh, but men are gradually learning to appreciate their mothers and their wives. Children are treated with more tenderness and their parents are beginning to enjoy the marvel of their gradual development. The material surfeit of the civilised world is unknown here, and small things bring great joy.

'The air of the caatinga is clear and dry, healthier than almost anywhere in Brazil, and we have no endemic diseases. The world is overcrowded and suffering from the resulting hysteria. Here we have a healthy land and a basically healthy people who love that land. No effort is too great to make our caatinga worth living in.'

26

HAVING decided that the struggle was worth while, the Padre concentrated on his tactics.

Transport was the most urgent need. The jeep, after devouring money for repairs, had finally collapsed and without one the work of the Fundação could not go on. Down in São Paulo a new jeep would cost about £900, but there was no money to pay for it. Finally, the Padre was obliged to buy one on the instalment system in Petrolina. The total cost of this would be £1,500 – a waste of about £600 for lack of ready cash.

The truck, too, was now an uneconomic proposition and had cost over £600 in repairs since January, besides the money lost by having to hire transport when it was out of action. A new truck would cost £2,500 but would save money in the long run. Since there was no money with which to buy it, the Padre was forced to continue with wasteful make-do-and-mend.

'I saw a sketch on television once,' he wrote. 'A poor man went to his bank manager to borrow money. "How much can you put down as security?" asked the manager. "Nothing," replied the man. "Well then, I am afraid we can't make you a loan." "But if I had money I wouldn't want to borrow it," said the poor fellow. "I see you only lend money to people who don't need it." I understand how he felt. Unless you have money, life is so very expensive.'

The Padre's immediate task was arranging to buy goats with the money sent from Cafod before shortage forced prices up still further. Until there was sufficient wild pasture it was no use bringing the animals to the area, as without tender greenstuff and some drinking water they would die in the early weeks.

Once acclimatised, they would adapt to the diet which sufficed for the local beasts.

So that the Padre travelled to Senhor do Bomfim in the neighbouring State of Bahia, where the most resistant strains of goats are bred and, with the help of the local priest, arranged with three different breeders for the purchase of 220 nanny goats and 30 males for delivery at the end of February should rain have fallen. Had the Fundação truck been in service and saved the extra cost of hiring two vehicles for delivery, 30% more goats could have been bought.

To distribute 250 goats amongst 1,500 families in an area where poverty is general is no easy task, but the Padre already had, as a basis, a census of all the flocks and herds in the area. He also knew almost every family personally.

Selection presented various problems. Poverty alone was no criterion. The ability of a man to make good use of his stock had to be taken into account, since this was not just a charitable operation but an opportunity for further development. The number of dependants also had to be considered, as well as the extent to which people had suffered from the drought.

Every family was questioned about their present situation. If the Padre's intentions had become known, he would have been besieged by people begging for animals, and wide-spread disappointment would have resulted. So the questions were asked in a friendly way without taking any notes at the time.

When the information was complete, 121 families were short-listed and from these, 50 were chosen and a number of goats allotted to each.

Padre Lira is firmly opposed to what he describes as 'paternalism' and he was resolved that each man should pay for the goats he received. In a country where money is hardly ever used it is difficult for a man to promise cash repayment. Even were money available, the progressive devaluation of the cruzeiro made a price fixed one year quite unrealistic the next.

After much thought, the Padre decided on repayment in

kind, and worked out an ingenious scheme. Each man would be given a form showing the terms of repayment for the four or five goats he would receive. Since billy goats were to cost, including the expense of transport, £7 each and nannies only £4.35, the Padre planned to make the money go further by arranging that neighbours or relations should share a male goat. Before receiving his animals, each man would be asked to agree to the terms applicable to himself.

Each of the recipients would repay one female goat at the end of the first year. The second year, those who had been allotted a billy goat would be responsible for returning a young male, and everyone would give one or two females, according to the number of goats they had started with. The third year, each family would repay two females. Since goats in the caatinga produce an average of 1.5 kids every year, this system would not prove onerous.

Should the head of a family die, the debt would be remitted. The goats returned would be used to form a revolving stock for future distribution.

Next, a number of points were chosen where people could most easily come to collect their goats when the day arrived, and a route was worked out for each of the two trucks.

On March 4th, three inches of rain fell, half filling the reservoir at the Fundação and providing valuable drinking water in the cisterns. Over part of the 'parish' rain continued, but at the Fundação, Curral Novo and Cacimbas sufficient grazing was not yet assured.

So Padre Lira went to Senhor do Bomfim once more and asked the breeders whether they would keep to the contract as arranged, but delay delivery until sufficient rain fell. Prices were rising all the time, and the men knew the uncertainty of the rainfall and of the date when they might get their money. They agreed, however. This was an anxious situation and besides, the question of Cafod's reaction to the long delay was preying on the Padre's mind.

Suddenly in April rain fell – more rain than in all the previous year. The reservoirs were overflowing. The caatinga was green. The trucks, loaded with goats, started on their journey and word was passed round that certain men should report at given points in two days' time.

The distribution, which was supervised by Candido, went smoothly and there was great rejoicing. 'I doubt whether anything we have done has had more impact,' wrote the Padre. 'We are profoundly grateful to Cafod.

'The men of the caatinga are deeply attached to their goats – not just because of their milk, butter, cheese and meat which feed the people, and the skins which are their surest form of income. Every animal has a name, and a catingueiro will spend days wandering through the scrub in search of a lost kid. The motherless young are brought into the house and petted by the children as if they were small brothers and sisters. This personal attachment is not typically Portuguese, but may come from early contact with the Indian tribes, who still lavish affection on their pet parrots, monkeys and other small animals.'

Although the grant from Christian Aid had been held up by the diversion of funds to East Pakistan, it would still have arrived in time for the goats destined for the pilot breeding project to be bought at the same time as those for Cafod. Unfortunately, however, the clearing banks, instead of sending the money to Juazeiro as directed, transferred it instead to Recife. Advice of its arrival was delayed, and it was July before the money could finally be collected. The caatinga was now dry and the project would have to be delayed for a whole year.

This pilot project was to form the basis of the communities which the Padre planned to establish as the second stage of his rural development.

'Through this land run a few semi-humid valleys following the course of the riachos,' he wrote. 'These valleys are overcrowded in terms of the life which they can support. Every father would like to leave his son "a piece of the river", as they say, but there comes a time when land can no longer be sub-divided.

'We must develop the empty land and start our communities wherever we can create a source of water. The Fundação owns some seven thousand acres of unused land and it is at various points on this that some of our pupils, now married, can make a start. As soon as the pilot goat-breeding project is established, the young people can learn rational methods of animal husbandry. They must be financed by means of loans with the Fundação acting initially as guarantor and accountant. The Government is encouraging rural development so arrangements should not be difficult to make. Ideally, these loans should be repaid as promptly as possible so that the young people become independent, but in any case, after a suitable proving period, they should be free to make their own financial arrangements.

'As the new methods are seen to be successful, so the older men will learn to imitate them and the whole standard of husbandry in the area will be raised. The next step will be the formation of co-operatives.'

On a brief trip to São Paulo in June the Padre collected 500 kilos of clothing and medicines, all of which were transported free to the Fundação. He was also given contributions totalling £272 for embroidery materials, as well as £90 for the purchase of tinned food for use in an emergency.

The children at Cacimbas who had begged so long for an embroidery class would at last have their wish, though as there was no building in which they could work, machine embroidery was out of the question. The girls would sit under the shade of the trees which had refreshed us on our visit to the hamlet.

'The main trouble is the wind, which blows dust onto their work,' wrote the Padre. 'But at least, fifty of the children will have made a start.

'Twenty-four pupils are learning machine embroidery at Fechadão and forty are working there by hand. We have come to the end of our stock of sewing-machines, so I took those from Curral Novo where old animosities still stifle the people's enthusiasm. The taste of the women there is poor, too, and the results of their work disappointing.'

I could not help remembering the plastic novelties in Seu José's house. If any of his womenfolk had a hand in choosing patterns and colours, the results would hardly be pleasing.

'With all these girls working, our supply of materials is running low once more. The Leigião Brasileira in Teresina has sent us £200 to be used for embroidery materials and £125 for community work and they promise us an equal amount next January,' the Padre explained.

'During the past school holidays Conçeição took a course in community development with the Leigião Brasileira and this work is now her concern. She visits the various hamlets and talks to the women and girls about hygiene and diet, and the care of children and so on.

'I have been shocked to find how little the girls here understand of the real meaning of marriage and its wonderful possibilities. Most brides embark on the married state with no understanding of marital sex relations. I must have been blind in the past, but it is not easy for a man. With Conceição they open up and begin to ask for explanations and advice. She is a born leader, but so gentle and kind that the women, and the children too, love her and listen to what she says.

'It is exhausting work. Sometimes, in order to take advantage of a trip which the jeep is making, Conceição has to travel as much as ten hours in one day over roads which you have sampled for yourself. At others, she remains for a week or more in a hamlet such as Cacimbas where the conditions are painfully uncomfortable. As she has to stay with one of the local families she must take food for herself and them, and here the tins from São Paulo come in very useful. Conceição is showing signs of fatigue and I don't feel justified in keeping her here when she should be getting married and setting up a home of her own.'

Muriel, meanwhile, had been passing through a time of crisis.

Several years previously, following a period of protracted ill health which sapped her confidence and made her feel more in need of shelter than at any time since her husband's death, she had become a Roman Catholic.

The years passed and gradually she felt a longing to return to the spiritual allegiance which had been so much part of her life as a country rector's wife. Only the fear that this change might handicap her work for the Padre caused her to postpone for some time the final step.

In the new climate of goodwill between the churches her decision met with understanding, on the whole, but she hesitated to tell the Padre of it in case this should cause him distress. Finally, however, she decided that to keep him in the dark would impair the intimacy of their relationship and so she wrote to him.

She need not have worried. On June 6th, 1971, the Padre replied, 'I don't understand why you are so concerned about your return to the Anglican Church. We must belong where we find peace, the peace of Christ who came to save us all, not just the Catholics, or the Anglicans or the Jews. I believe, and I hope I am not wrong, that true religion is within us. If we are honest with ourselves, fulfil the obligations to which we are called and love our neighbours, then we love God and God accepts our love, whatever the religion to which we hold.

'We are living in a period of transition, of profound religious, social, scientific and ideological change. In this confused world, if we cannot be at peace with ourselves we merely increase the multitude of the rebellious, the misfits and the unbelieving. May you, dear mother, be at peace with your conscience and that is enough. Your prayers will always be for me a source of strength.'

27

SOME doubt had arisen whether Peter Oakley would return to Brazil after his leave in England, so the Padre was delighted when, on May 1st, he arrived at the Fundação in the Cessna.

Peter brought the good news that Oxfam had made a grant of £3,000 for new reservoirs and it was decided that the work could be carried out in about two months.

The Director of Oxfam, Leslie Kirkley, was to tour Latin America in October and the Padre asked whether he could visit the Fundação for the inauguration of the shoe factory and see all that had been done with Oxfam's help. Peter promised to put the matter up, and at once the Padre began to plan a Concentração on a far greater scale than the one which we had attended. The Prefect of São Raimundo would be asked to contribute to the expense. A thousand horsemen would ride in. The Governor of Piauí would be a guest of honour. All the people round about would be drawn into a great communal effort and given something wonderful to remember after the bleak months of the drought. The Padre's eyes shone.

Two hours later Peter flew back to Juazeiro. The airstrip was a wonderful link with the outside world.

A month later he returned with Lucy Fowke, whom he had met some time before through the wife of another Oxfam representative. They were to be married that evening at Santo Sé, a village on the far side of the São Francisco River.

Peter told the Padre that Oxfam planned further help with reservoirs and would be sending another £1,000 for famine relief. The money would be transferred via the Bishop of Juazeiro.

'One of the finest bishops in Latin America,' commented the Padre. 'He has been a very good friend to us.'

The question of the teachers' salaries was once more causing anxiety. The previous year the Governor of Piauí had only paid ten of the twelve months promised, and before the end of his term of office had refused to renew the grant.

This year, the total of the salaries had increased since Ponta da Serra, with sixty pupils, had been added to the list of schools, and there were still over a hundred children waiting in the expectation that a school would be opened at Ladeira if the necessary money could be found.

The Padre's only hope, when dealing with officials, was to go himself and present his case. Methodical as always, he kept an exact list of his journeys, together with their cost, as these had to be included in his often abortive applications for grants. During the three years from 1968 to 1970, he had been absent from the Fundação on essential journeys for 175, 160 and 142 days respectively, travelling for a large part of the time in conditions of great discomfort. To make things worse, more than half of these journeys had been fruitless.

If the new Governor of Piauí would come to the Concentração in October and see for himself what had been achieved at the Fundação perhaps things would be easier in future. To the Padre's great satisfaction his invitation was accepted.

School buildings were another urgent necessity for which help had been promised, though not given, by the previous Governor.

'If we could get the money to start building at Cacimbas where the need, as you have seen for yourself, is so great,' the Padre wrote, 'I feel that the authorities would provide the funds for completing it. I have heard it maintained that the charitable institutions of Brazil just sit around and wait for Government help. If this were the case, most of us would long ago have ceased to exist.

'You questioned my estimate of £1,800 for building the Cacimbas school, Dona Peggie. We have only a simple building in mind, but I assure you that this estimate is reasonable. The further north one goes in Brazil the more everything costs, and there is the additional expense of bringing materials and skilled labour from the towns to the building site.'

The Fundação was turning into a small hamlet. The building where we had stayed was now enlarged to include three more bedrooms, showers and three W.C.'s, store rooms for food, medicines, educational equipment and linen, supplies from Caritas, and shoes awaiting sale. There was also a small shop where the people of the Fundação could buy food and necessities at cost price. The old lean-to kitchen still had to serve until money was available to replace it with something more modern, but there was now a small bakehouse to relieve some of the pressure on cooking space.

For years the Padre had been hoping to build houses instead of the huts used during term time by mothers of school children who lived at a great distance. The question of accommodation for the apprentices was also becoming urgent.

Twenty tons of food no longer required by a Sudene work front had been obtained through the good offices of Robert Standley of USAID Recife. With this food and the Oxfam money, the Padre was able to arrange for the building of twelve small houses, keeping a large number of men employed and their families fed.

One of the new buildings was to house the apprentices in the shoe factory and another, the girls who carried out the more delicate tasks such as glueing the linings.

The factory had been at a standstill for weeks because no technician could be found who would face the drought. It was clear that in order to achieve continuity one of the apprentices, accustomed from birth to the harsh local conditions, must be trained to take over the supervision of the factory and the maintenance of the machinery. If the boy who was chosen were to remain too long in the south, he might be tempted to settle there, so the Padre planned that he should learn as much as possible whilst still at the Fundação and then go to Franca only for a short finishing course.

In July, thanks to the good offices of Senhor Silvio, one of the most influential men in the shoe-making industry, a new technician arrived. He was only twenty-four, but extremely competent, and output soon rose to a hundred pairs of shoes a day. He suggested that they should expand production to include a simple type of shoe which could be sold all the year round for rougher wear by grown-ups as well as children. Also that by using more modern methods and new lasts and jigs, production costs could be cut by 30%, and he advised the Padre to go to Franca and negotiate the purchase of the necessary equipment, which would soon pay for itself.

Each pair of shoes was now stamped in gold with the trade mark, 'Calçados Muriel' and wrapped in a blue plastic bag marked in the same way.

Amongst the apprentices was a boy called João de Deus who, besides showing special aptitude with the machinery as well as the shoe-making techniques, was enthusiastic and conscientious. The technician set to work to train him as a future overseer.

Many of the apprentices were hoping to get married but waiting patiently until they could have a house of their own. However one of them, a boy named Batista, decided on a runaway match and appeared with his bride at the Fundação. For months he had saved up the five pounds a month paid to him – a fortune in these parts – and prepared for a wedding breakfast.

'Everyone who was able gave them a present,' wrote the Padre, 'a blanket, plates, a frying pan and all sorts of things for the kitchen. The professoras, too, each gave them a *lembrança*, and now the couple have set up house beneath a tree. It is very touching.'

News had reached us that, for the first time in history, a Brazilian Government was resolved to tackle the problems of the Cinderella State. 'PIAUÍ EXISTS', announced the newspaper headlines. There was talk of the 'Projeto Piauí', a plan to raise the standard of living in the whole State. It was to be divided into regions, each with a team of technicians who would carry out surveys and devise an economic infrastructure for the future.

Plans were under discussion for an important irrigation scheme in the Gurgueia Valley. On hearing of these the Padre wrote, 'I was born in the valley and for the last thirty years I have been convinced that it will one day be the granary of the North-East. The soil is fertile and, unlike the neighbouring agreste, there is an abundance of water, but it has never been properly exploited. Everyone wanted me to locate the Fundação there, but this was not my plan. One day someone was bound to develop such a favoured region, but no one would tackle the desolate caatinga.'

Another great scheme was under way to dam the São Francisco River above Juazeiro and form a lake which would submerge the highway over which we had travelled from Petrolina towards Remanso. This would push the main road some twenty kilometres nearer the low hills which formed the border of the State of Piauí.

Dams have sometimes had unforeseen and most unwelcome side effects, but in this case, the formation of a large body of water in such an arid area must surely be to the good and might even have a favourable effect on the climate of the caatinga. Navigation would carry on as before, and as the river was already dammed at Paulo Afonso the lower reaches would not be threatened in any way.

The 'Projeto Piauí' was at a very early stage, but even the fact that plans were being made was encouraging. Wholesale industrialisation, which has destroyed the quality of life in so many regions, did not appear to be a threat in view of the climate and the low density of the population. But whatever the future should hold, it was clear that education was required if the people were to benefit.

'Literacy is an essential step in the development of the backward regions,' wrote the Padre, 'but the problem, tackled in the conventional manner, is too big for any government to solve in one generation. Abortive experiments in the past have shown this, but they have also indicated the reasons for their failure.

'The population density in the backward areas does not warrant the establishment of permanent schools. Moreover, where poverty is general, parents cannot afford to dispense with the labour of their children for long periods at a time and therefore start with a prejudice against schooling.

'If the teacher is not properly trained the children make no progress, the parents lose any interest they may have had, and the pupils drift away. Indeed, if the school is ill-equipped and cheerless, there is nothing which makes them want to stay.

'Education is not a dish of gruel which one sets before a starving man in the certainty that he will devour it. Ignorant people may feel no urge to learn. In order that they shall make the effort you must arouse their interest.

'The first requirement is for properly trained and enthusiastic teachers, but there are not enough girls of the right calibre who are prepared to spend several years in the discomfort and isolation of the sertão. Nor are funds available to pay a large number of such teachers the salary to which they are entitled.

'During the long journeys and in the quiet hours of the night I have thought about this problem and I am convinced that the solution lies in mobile schools.

'After deciding on suitable points, a team of young teachers would visit each in turn for a period of two months in order to give an intensive course in the three R's. The team would arrive in a lorry bringing a tent for sleeping, one for daytime use, a mobile kitchen and a portable W.C. and shower. A small generator would be a useful addition, though this is not absolutely necessary.

'Besides the driver, there would be another person to help with setting up the unit, servicing the equipment and cooking the meals. The team would bring its own supplies of food as well as raw materials for school meals.

'It would also be equipped with educational material, posters and a loudspeaker to broadcast music as well as announcements. The Brazilian flag would be hoisted, as well as that of any organisation or group which might have participated in the experiment.

'People living in isolation welcome any chance for getting together – even a funeral – and the two months stay of a team would be an occasion for meetings, dances, competitions and demonstrations of various skills or procedures. It would be a happy time for everyone.

'With lively young teachers and proper instruction, the children would make more progress in two months than in a year or more of the dismal schools which have existed here and there in the past. The team would leave a supply of material for continued practice in reading and writing, and would explain to the brighter pupils how they could help the others. From time to time, the team would return to each place for a short refresher course.

'Word would be sent round well in advance inviting people to come and enjoy this opportunity for social activities, and this would be an initial step towards the formation of a community spirit and later, of co-operatives.

'I have talked to a number of young teachers and all of them agreed they would be happy to volunteer for an enterprise where they would be pioneers working as a group in conditions which, though adventurous, offered reasonable living conditions.

'The truck and equipment could be marked "Mobile School Service" and the girls might like to wear an attractive uniform with a corresponding badge.

'Under the leadership of the present government the young have been fired with a wish to go out into the backward areas of our country and help to develop their great potential. I feel sure that they would make an enthusiastic response to a plan for a mobile literacy campaign.'

Water conservation was still one of the main problems, both of the Fundação and of the whole caatinga. During our enquiries we had come upon a very interesting system devised by the

Intermediate Technology Development Group (ITDG), which made use of unskilled labour. It consisted, essentially, of filling plastic tubes with a moist mixture of sand and cement so as to form sausages which, before they hardened, could be bent to take any required shape. The filling of these was so simple that it could be undertaken even by school children.

A reservoir would have to be sited at the base of a slope which would serve as a catchment. After digging a pit with sloping sides, this would be lined with heavy-duty plastic in order to form a completely watertight skin over the porous ground beneath. To protect this layer, the floor and sides would be lined with 'sausages' placed in position before they hardened. Various methods of roofing, such as brushwood laid on wires, or wire netting covered with dried foliage had been tried. In view of the high winds of the caatinga any such covering would need to be securely held in place.

Another most ingenious system devised by ITDG is to construct on the floor of a pit lined with polythene a large number of hollow bee-hives, also made with 'sausages'. One of these is made taller than the rest and has an open top. The depression is then filled with sand and levelled off.

When rain falls it percolates down through the sand and forces its way into the bee-hives, thus forming a collection of underground water pockets. The projecting open-topped container acts as a well. As water is drawn off from it, more enters the remaining hives. Evaporation is almost nil with this method and the water is automatically filtered. Moreover, it is protected from pollution by animals. The system could be used on a small scale, at very low cost, to serve individual families.

I also came upon an interesting account in a newspaper of a 'desert still', which had been used to produce up to a litre of water a day in such unpromising spots as the Sahara and the Gobi Desert. Its effectiveness depended upon a considerable difference in temperature between night and day, and all the equipment needed was a plastic sheet and rubber tubing. The device was suggested as a piece of survival technique and should prove very handy in times of drought, or even to produce some sweet drinking water where the only available supply was saline.

During the summer, the Padre wrote that his uncle Alcibiades was suffering from cataract and would have to undergo an operation.

'He has devoted sons and daughters in Rio and will be well cared for. He wants to come back, but I know they will not let him return. He is an old man now. You will be glad to hear that we did not cut down his tree.'

We had heard nothing from Padre Lorenz for over two years and Padre Lira was anxious because he had had no news either. Now, a letter arrived from Brazil with an unexpected report, 'our mutual friend has become a chaplain in the leprosarium near the gas works in Rio and seems at last very contented.'

'I am not surprised,' commented Padre Lira when we wrote to him with this news. 'In one of those fits of depression which sometimes overwhelmed him, the Padre told me that he would end his days with the lepers and that once this decision was taken, none of us would ever hear from him again.'

28

SINCE the Padre believes that any opportunity of bringing his people together and uniting them in communal effort is of value, he determined that the Concentração should be held on as large a scale as possible. Weeks before October 9th, the great day, word had been going round, and it seemed that about a thousand riders would gather with members of their families to see the Governor of Piauí and join in thanking Leslie Kirkley, the Director of Oxfam, for the benefits which they had all shared.

Notables from the whole district had been invited and these, with their wives and the guests of honour, sixty-eight people in all, would sit down to lunch in the recreation hall. The Padre's sister Mercês from Ceará had volunteered to organise the meal, and the school children were busy practising songs to provide incidental music during the meal.

The Padre reckoned that, apart from those served in the hall, at least 2,000 meals would be needed. He accordingly arranged with five volunteer cooks to come from São Raimundo the day before, each with a team of half a dozen helpers. Five of the family houses would be used as kitchens and everything but the rice prepared beforehand. The four steers and ten pigs contributed by friends were slaughtered. China, glass and cutlery given by factory owners in São Paulo were already stored in sufficient quantity.

This was to be the greatest festa in the history of the Fundação. Unfortunately, with the growing heat, the season was not propitious and the grazing for the riders' mounts already scorched and uneatable. However, the date had to be chosen to fit in with Leslie Kirley's tour of Latin America, and it was a measure of the people's interest that they were willing to undertake the arduous journey.

In the midst of all these preparations news arrived that Leslie Kirkley had been obliged to cancel his tour as Oxfam was diverting all its energies to raising funds for Pakistan. The Padre felt that it was his duty immediately to inform the Governor who nevertheless replied that it was his intention to attend the Concentração. There was a general foreboding that he might not, after all, arrive and many people, feeling that the occasion had lost its glamour, decided not to come. Programmes had already been printed. The Bishop of Juazeiro had agreed to lend his aeroplanes to bring V.I.P.'s from Petrolina, and without post or telephone it is very difficult to put arrangements into reverse.

On the day, arrangements worked smoothly. As the guests reached a point about a kilometre from the Fundação on each of the two approach roads, all but those who had been invited to the hall received tickets showing to which of the family houses they should go for their meals.

Promptly at ten the Cessna arrived, bringing Peter Oakley and his wife Lucy. The Governor, as had been feared, did not appear, but sent a representative.

As at the previous Concentração, the horsemen charged into the compound. There was a ceremony as the flags, including the Union Jack, were hoisted. Peter Oakley made a speech from a platform set up in front of the school building and the factory was declared to be formally inaugurated.

At twelve o'clock 1,324 meals were served to ticket holders and by one o'clock everyone had eaten. A great deal of food was left and this was divided between people for the journey home, which might last as long as two or three days.

A portrait of Muriel, as patron of the Fundação was unveiled after the meal, but when the Padre was telling his audience that this was someone whom he regarded as a mother, his voice failed him.

'The meal was enjoyed by everyone,' he wrote. 'It was cooked with plenty of pork fat and after weeks of dry and tasteless food it is a wonderful treat to have something which is really rich. Unhappily, as always happens at a festa, a number of people were ill afterwards, but I am sure they felt it had been worth while.

'In spite of our disappointments it was a great day, and we had an important visitor, Senhor João Ribeiro, who has been entrusted by the Federal Government with planning for the Projeto Piauí. He declared himself impressed with what he saw and announced that he would be returning to the area for a preliminary survey in January or February.

'Your visit in 1968 was more simple, no guests of honour and no formal speeches, but it was so much happier. Then it was a family occasion with human warmth.'

Later he wrote, 'I am overwhelmed with work, but I know that your questions are important, Dona Peggie, so I will answer them quickly. You ask if I wish to revise my last list of priorities. As you know, apart from the reservoirs, transport has always been, and remains, highest on the list.

'Next to this, I feel, must come a means of rapid communication. If some disaster should occur here and, as so frequently happens, our transport is laid up, all we can do is take a horse and ride – 204 kilometres to Juazeiro and Petrolina or 120 kilometres to São Raimundo. During the rainy season our way may even be blocked by swollen riachos.

'The big landowners in other parts of Brazil use radio transceivers in order to keep in touch with their estates. These sets are quite simple, adjusted to communicate between two fixed points at a certain hour of the day. With such an apparatus and our airstrip we should have a life-line, and this would take a tremendous weight off my mind.

'One of my chief preoccupations is still the number of women who die in childbirth. Apart from lacking medical care, they are often weakened by malnutrition and unable to withstand what, in normal circumstances, would be no more than a simple accident of childbirth. As long as food is available, I am giving a small ration to pregnant women, but they need pre-natal care, as well as assistance in the case of difficult births.

'In the village of Lagoa do Alegre just over the Bahia border, the Bishop of Juazeiro has set up a maternity unit which is saving countless lives. If we could have something on a much smaller scale – just a simple building with basic equipment – I know of a competent woman who is ready to take over the midwifery duties.'

I accordingly wrote to the Head of the Order of Malta in Rome who had been Austrian Minister when we were there in the early 'fifties. In his reply, Prince Schwarzenberg suggested that I should get in touch with the Chancellor of the Order's association in Rio, Ambassador Pio Correa. Through his kind offices, I was put in touch with Minister Grieco of the Brazilian Embassy in London, who lost no time in drawing the attention of General Veloso, Secretary General of the Ministry of the Interior in Brasilia, to the Padre's project and his needs. A few days later a telegram arrived to say that the irrigation needs of the Fundação would be discussed with Peter Stern of the Intermediate Technology Development Group who was then on an exploratory visit to the North-East.

The work of the Fundação was becoming known, but each new contact added to the Padre's burden of desk work.

'I have to leave for Teresina in mid-November,' he wrote. 'The Leigião Brasileira is organising a sale of our embroidery together with a display of our shoes. While I am in Teresina I plan to organise a store and sales outlet for our shoes. We can no longer cope with the increasing stocks at the Fundação.

'Before I leave there are reports to write for Caritas, Oxfam and Cafod. All the embroidery must be priced and the pupils' credit accounts made up. The bank is pressing for a valuation of all the Fundação property as security for our loans. The State Secretary of Education has at last signed an agreement to pay about £125 a month towards the professoras' salaries, beginning next year, but in order to do this he must have a report and statistics.

'Then there is Christian Aid. Everything is now ready for the pilot project except the goats, which cannot be brought here until after the rains.

'The doctor keeps insisting that I must not work by lamp-light, but it is impossible to follow his advice. I am obliged to work in the evenings and we cannot afford to keep the generator going when the factory does not need it.

'If only Candido could help me with all this. He has the will but not the capacity. If devotion could supply the education he lacks, I should have the finest assistant in the world.

'Candido, as I told you, is like a son. He confides in me and sometimes I give him advice. He has a girl friend in Remanso, a very intelligent young woman who has taken courses in community development. If they get married she will be a wonderful asset to the Fundação. However he does not seem very enthusiastic and seldom visits her. Much as I would like to, I am not trying to influence him. This is something which he must work out for himself.

'Today I had a letter from Alcibiades. The operation on his right eye was successful and the other eye will be treated in January. Life in Rio is meaningless, he says, and he would like to return here and die with us. His tree will be waiting for him.'

The story goes on. Thirteen years of struggle and continuous overwork have eroded the Padre's physical resistance, but they have only strengthened his spirit.

He set out with two simple aims – to enable his people to remain secure on their land, and to make the quality of their lives worth while. Just as he had to build roads to open up the land, so he has had to make his own paths through a sociologically unexplored territory.

The natural forces opposing him were tremendous: drought, desolation and distance. These he knew and accepted. They were the challenge and he has found the means to conquer them.

The apathy, ignorance and suspicion of the catingueiros were also known to him before he began his work. Hope deferred and broken promises were unexpected and hard to bear.

The world is changing fast and the countries which have lagged behind are often those which make the fastest strides. In Brazil now an adventurous spirit of social service is growing up amongst the young and there are men of goodwill and immense drive in the Government. It is to be hoped that they will provide the basic support needed for the Fundação, which is a blue print for development all over a region hitherto considered to be without hope.

Whatever the outcome of planning by the Brazilian Government, the Padre will always need the support of his friends at home and abroad, and the warmth of their human concern.

GLOSSARY

Only the meanings used in the text have been given in the following list. Many others will be found in the dictionary.

abraço: a gesture of greeting between friends which varies from a pat on the shoulder to a hug

agreste: area of North-East Brazil which, though dry, will produce crops

angico: a tree with a thorny trunk. Yields a sweet resin

Bandeirantes: members of early expeditions from São Paulo into the interior

caatinga: area of arid scrubland in North-East Brazil

catingueiro: inhabitant of the caatinga

caboclo: a half-breed

cachaça: a spirit made from sugar cane

cafezinho: small cup of black coffee drunk at frequent intervals in Brazil

candomblé: north-eastern version of the religion brought to Brazil by the African slaves

carijó: a breed of speckled hen

Carioca: an inhabitant of Rio de Janeiro

caroá: plant of the pineapple family with spiky leaves

concentração: a gathering of people

curandeiro: a folk healer

desobriga: annual visit from the priest which gives people the opportunity to discharge their obligations to the Church

dignidade: self-respect

facheiro: candelabra cactus

favela: vulture nettle or giant euphorbia

feijoada: stew made from meat, black beans and seasoning

festa: festival

Festas da Patria: national day of celebration

figueira: evergreen tree with brightgreen leaves

flagelados: victims of the drought; literally, 'the scourged'

juazeiro: tall tree with dark evergreen leaves
lembrança: keepsake, present
linguiça: salami-type of rough sausage
lobisomem: were-wolf
macambira: a bromeliad
malagueta: tiny, very hot peppers
mãe ingleza: English mother
mandacarú: a tree cactus branching out from a central stem
mato: scrub country; the brush
merenda: a light meal
mucambé: a medicinal plant
mucunã: leguminous plant
muito prazer: corresponds to the English 'How-do-you-do?'
onça: animal of the cat tribe, wild cat
parasita: parasitic climbing plant
Piauiense: native of Piauí
quema: runaway match (north-eastern dialect)
rezas: witches
riacho: seasonal watercourse
seriema: the crested seriema
sertão: the backland
Seu: colloquial form of Senhor
tapioca: manioc starch
tiquira: alcoholic drink made from manioc
tropeiro: muleteer
umburana: large tree with resinous bark and leaves which can be used to make an infusion for influenza
umbuzeiro: tree bearing small fruit like grapes
vereador: title sometimes used for the most important member of a small community
xique-xique: cactus with long white spines, which branches straight out from the ground